THE WORLD ACCORDING TO CYCLES

THE WORLD ACCORDING TO CYCLES

How Recurring Forces Can Predict the Future
and Change Your Life

Samuel A. Schreiner, Jr.

Skyhorse Publishing

Skyhorse Publishing books may be purchased in bulk at special discounts for sales promotion, corporate gifts, fund-raising, or educational purposes. Special editions can also be created to specifications. For details, contact the Special Sales Department, Skyhorse Publishing, 555 Eighth Avenue, Suite 903, New York, NY 10018 or info@skyhorsepublishing.com.

www.skyhorsepublishing.com

10 9 8 7 6 5 4 3 2 1

Library of Congress Cataloging-in-Publication Data

Schreiner, Samuel Agnew.
The world according to cycles : how recurring forces can predict the future and change your life / Samuel A. Schreiner, Jr.
p. cm.
ISBN 978-1-60239-646-3 (hardcover : alk. paper)
1. Cycles. 2. Forecasting. 3. Self-help techniques. I. Title.
B105.C9S37 2009
116--dc22
2009013561

Printed in the United States of America

For Dorrie, who went cycling with me, and for
Beverly and Carolyn, who made this book possible. . . .

CONTENTS

AN INTRODUCTION TO CYCLES

There is ample evidence that mankind has been acutely aware of how cycles can influence human life from the time that the race evolved into thinking creatures. The most primitive people lived, consciously or unconsciously, by the cycles of seasons, of night and day, of tides and weather, of pulse and breathing. Artifacts like Stonehenge in Britain, dating from somewhere between 3000 and 1500 B.C., and the structures in Central America that enabled creation of the Mayan Calendar in 300 B.C. show how long people have attempted to read the celestial cycles for earthly guidance. How far we have come in this endeavor over all these years is demonstrated most dramatically by moon landings and space flights but most usefully by that vocalizing gadget in an ordinary automobile that tells the driver where to turn next on the way to the supermarket.

What is new with respect to the place of cycles in human thought and activity is the development in less than a current lifetime of a system of thought—a science, in fact—based on the study of cycles that are being discovered as active agents in everything from the tiny atom to the whole wide universe. These studies are providing not only better navigational guidance but directions on how and when it is best to invest in the stock market, come in out of the rain, take medications, exercise, work, rest, and relax—in short, to control a life. By definition, cycles are rhythmic, recurring in equal time spans, and thus serve as a predictive device. Cycle students have been using this device in very practical and profitable ways, such as taking advantage of stock market fluctuations or building homes away from cyclical flooding or earthquake areas.

During a reporter's investigation into what might be called cycleland, the author was impressed by examples of how cycle study had eased or enriched or, in some cases, saved lives. But I was even more impressed to learn how discovering cycles had changed and enlarged minds. "There's just a feeling that some of us get that we are touching something far beyond what we have been aware of or conscious of," one lifelong cycles student said, while another claimed that through cycles "the universe is shown to be an even more marvelous place than hitherto realized." Although it humbles a person to acknowledge that he or she cannot control a world according to cycles, it is energizing to realize that it is a world of order and predictability in which knowledge makes it possible to prosper by adapting to its rhythms. My purpose in writing this book is to introduce readers to a world that I find both fascinating and comforting.

—Samuel A. Schreiner, Jr.

Chapter 1

What *Everything* Is About

When I first discovered the world of cycles twenty years ago, I asked Dr. Jeffrey Horovitz, then director of a still unique organization, the Foundation for the Study of Cycles, why he had given up the practice of psychiatry to concentrate on cycles. His enthusiasm for the work was so strong that he could not sit still while he answered. Pacing the floor and waving his arms as if taking in the whole of the universe, he said, "There's just a feeling that some of us get that we are touching something far beyond what we have been aware of or conscious of. It's that feeling of making discoveries like in second grade when you realize you can read. The hair starts to stand up on the back of your neck. You get a different sense of what *everything* is about."

On New Zealander Roy Tomes's Web site, you can find an equally arresting explanation as to why cycle thinking lured him away from a career in computers to work with cycles:

There are cycles in everything. There are cycles in the weather, the economy, the Sun, wars, geological formations, atomic vibrations, climate, human moods, the motions of planets, populations of animals, the occurrence of diseases, the prices of commodities and shares, and the large-scale structure of the universe. None of these are independent of each other. Research shows that very different disciplines often find the same cycle periods in their data. The interrelatedness of all things is an idea whose time has come. The study of cycles is an excellent way to understand this because the periods of cycles are as easy to recognize as fingerprints or DNA sequences.

In twenty years, Dr. Horovitz's sense that cycles may explain everything has changed to Tomes's confident claim that they already explain something very important—the interrelatedness of all things. This comes close to claiming that cycle thinkers have the elusive goal in sight that physicist Stephen J. Hawking called "the ultimate theory of the universe" in *A Brief History of Time*. Hawking writes that "ever since the dawn of civilization, people have not been content to see events as unconnected and inexplicable. They have craved an understanding of the underlying order in the world. Today we still yearn to know why we are here and where we came from. Humanity's deepest desire for knowledge is justification enough for our continuing quest. And our goal is nothing less than a complete description of the universe we live in."

Physicists such as Hawking have made a strong case for the fact that we live in a moving world. The book in your hand, the chair you are sitting in, the glasses perched on your nose are in constant motion. Unsettling as the thought may be, there is no such thing as solid matter; there are

waves in matter's tiniest particle. You may react to this assertion as I would
have reacted before discovering cycles, as the British author Samuel Johnson reacted 300 years ago. When confronted with his contemporary Bishop
Berkeley's philosophy stating matter exists only in a person's conception of
it, Johnson kicked a heavy stone and said, "I refute it thus." The rather
recent discoveries of science would suggest that Bishop Berkeley was closer
to the truth than Dr. Johnson. A popular book, *The Secret,* quotes physicist
Dr. Fred Alan Wolf as reporting that, "quantum physics really begins to
point to this discovery. It says that you can't have a universe without mind
entering into it, and that the mind is actually shaping the very thing that is
being perceived."

If everything we perceive as solid moves, understanding how—and, if
possible, why—things move is essential to understanding life itself and how
we can make the best use of it. This is the quest of people studying cycles,
and they have gone a long way in a very short time. This is not to say that an
awareness of the existence and importance of cycles is a new discovery. But
we tend to take cycles for granted as our reliance upon them is as essential to
life as breathing, a cycle in itself. Perhaps the most obvious of the vital cycles
outside of our own bodies to which we seldom give a thought is the rising of
the Sun, or, more accurately, the turning of the Earth. We are able to predict
confidently and truly that morning will follow night simply because it has
been so for all of our recorded history and, from what we have been able to
learn, for all of the millions upon millions of years before our own creation.
Because all life—which, in human beings, includes the mind as well as the

body—is so profoundly influenced by this cycle of light and dark, what about the nature and uses of other cycles?

Since the times of Tao in China, Ecclesiastes in Jerusalem, Plato in Greece, Buddha in India, Virgil in Rome, philosophers, poets, and prophets have speculated about this question. Now the scientists are joining them. The identification and descriptions of cycles range through all disciplines— biology, geology, astrology, chemistry, physics, mathematics, psychology, economics, political science. So far, according to the files in the Foundation for the Study of Cycles, in Albuquerque, New Mexico, some 7,000 cycles have been discovered with more emerging almost every day. Gradually, the mesh of these separate cycles, like the gears in an intricate machine, is becoming evident through increased awareness of their function. The way you feel today, for example, can be traced through these many cycles to the trajectory of a far star.

The Foundation did not come into being through the philosophical musings of some stargazer or poet; it was born of necessity in the practical mind of a Harvard-educated economist named Edward R. Dewey who was asked to look into the causes of the Great Depression while working for the Commerce Department in the Hoover Administration. Searching for an answer, Dewey left the government to work for Chapin Hoskins, a former managing editor of *Forbes*, who was selling his analyses of business cycles to industry. Dewey had to learn about cycles to persuade clients of the need for Hoskins's services. In the course of this effort, Dewey came across an account of an international conference on biological cycles held in 1931 at the summer camp of Boston financier Copley Amory in Matamek, Quebec.

Some of the cycles in living things such as Canadian lynx, snowshoe rabbits, and Atlantic salmon looked enough like cycles in the markets to raise an intriguing question in Dewey's mind: Might not all cycles come from the same source? The more he thought about it, the more Dewey felt that this was a question in need of an answer, and the only way to find that answer would be to study the whole range of cycles.

Dewey wrote to Amory proposing a foundation for this study and received an enthusiastic response. Not only did Amory put up $500 in seed money but he agreed to serve as chairman of the Foundation, and in this capacity he helped recruit a distinguished executive committee. Among its members were Dr. Julian S. Huxley, secretary of the Zoological Society of London; Dr. Harlow Shapley, director of the Harvard Observatory; and Alanson B. Houghton, chairman of the Corning Glass Works and a former ambassador to Germany. As director of the Foundation, Dewey parted company with Hoskins but not with economic cycles. In order to fund his operations, Dewey continued to sell research to corporations, publishing general information he encountered about cycles. This method of operation left much to be desired. The saleable economic research took most of Dewey's working time. Dewey's clients didn't want the research published as they worried their competitors would glean it for free. By 1950, with his own curiosity about cycles as a universal phenomenon increasing, Dewey decided to take a gamble by leaving commerce and turning the Foundation into a nonprofit membership organization free to pursue and publish whatever was relevant to its mission.

Dewey ran his Foundation from New York but soon moved it to Pittsburgh where his chief researcher, Gertrude Shirk, was already at work and where he could be near the ancestral estate at Brady's Bend, Pennsylvania, that he inherited. There the Foundation remained, quietly accumulating cycles, publishing two magazines, *Cycles* and the *Journal of Interdisciplinary Cycle Research*, and a number of books. Dewey was the Foundation's director and guiding light until his death in 1978. Although Shirk stayed in place, leadership passed through a number of hands, and by the time I discovered cycles, in 1989, Dr. Horovitz had taken over. I found him and his crew in Irvine, California, a move made easier by the fact that Shirk elected to retire. In 1989, Dr. Horovitz left the Foundation to pursue other interests, and Richard Mogey took over until his retirement in 1997. There was a troubled period during which the Foundation ceased to function until president and director David Perales resurrected it in Albuquerque, New Mexico, as a much needed resource in the new millennium.

Defining the subject of cycle studies has been an ongoing task for the Foundation. Definitions can be difficult. Gertrude Stein postulated an interesting way of defining something: "a rose is a rose is a rose." If I read her right, she means that a rose, or anything else, is unique. William Shakespeare said much the same when he wrote "a rose by any other name would smell as sweet." Although a major objective of cycles studies is to show that they are as definite and recognizable as roses, a complete definition of this phenomenon is somewhat elusive. This is not to say that there are not valid guidelines for recognizing a cycle when you see one or experience its effects.

As the founder of what he called "the science of cycles," Dewey offered this fairly straightforward definition of the subject: "*Cycle* comes from a Greek word for 'circle.' Actually, the word *cycle* means 'coming around again to the place of the beginning.' It does not, by itself, imply that there is a regular period of time before it returns to the place where it started. When there is such a fairly regular period of time, the correct word to use is *rhythm*, from another Greek word meaning 'measured time.' Tides are rhythmic; your heartbeat is rhythmic; so is your breathing. A cycle when we refer to one, will usually mean a cycle with rhythm." Accordingly, he stated that the business of the science of cycles was to deal with "events that occur with reasonable regularity," whether they could be found in nature or commercial activity or anywhere else.

In a sense, Dr. Horovitz echoed Dewey when he told me, "Cycle by definition means circle—one complete turn of the circle until you get back to the same spot on the circle." Then Dr. Horotvitz quickly added, "The circles we look at are not particularly round, and when you show them like frequencies they are not necessarily sine waves. When the Foundation was started the definition was periodic rhythmic fluctuations. Now we have come to realize that there are recurring patterns that you can identify and that there are systems based on them, including human behavior."

It is evident that it would be a mistake to visualize cycles exclusively as either perfect circles or smoothly undulating waves. The most distinguishing feature of a true cycle is statistically significant regularity. Except for the self-evident natural ones such as the twenty-four-hour cycle of a day, it often takes rigorous and extensive examination to detect this all-important feature of a cycle. Because even true cycles manifest themselves in an infinite variety of shapes, sizes, and rhythms, it is easy to be deceived by recurrences that appear to have a cyclical character but may only be accidents or coincidences. As an example of this, Gary Bosley, former managing director of the Foundation, cited intriguing circumstances surrounding the 1989 Kentucky Derby. At 44 degrees, it was the coldest race day since 1957; it was the slowest since 1958; and there was a winning horse from California as in 1958. In those previous years there was a sunspot high as there was in 1989; the thirty-one- and thirty-two-year time stretch represents approximately three eleven-year sunspot cycles. Bosley shrugged off the derby events as coincidence at the time of our talk. These circumstances coincided only twice which is not enough to suspect there is a cycle at work, but it does not rule out the possibility of further confirming recurrences.

Even established regularity is not enough to precisely define a cycle. The most regular of cycles are subject to confusing changes. One example—a cycle, as Dewey said, "to keep scientists humble"—was a 40.68-month cycle in industrial common stock prices that kept the same shape between 1871 and 1946, through many economic crises and two world wars, only to do a complete reversal. After faltering briefly, the cycle returned to a forty-one month rhythm in the 1950s, but it traced a mirror image of its behavior on the graph. At least one convincing reason for this is postulated by cycle students: There is no such thing as a single cycle.

"When we study any system, whether it is the stock market or animal populations or rainfall or temperatures or earthquakes with our mathematical tests, we find that most characteristic systems have a number of characteristic cycles within them," Dr. Horovitz explains:

> Sometimes all the cycles peak at the same time and create a tremendous high; sometimes they bottom at the same time to make a tremendous low. At other times they cause frequency interferences like static in a radio signal. When they interfere with each other, cycles give you the total mathematical addition or subtraction of their different influences.
>
> Take tides, which may be the greatest example of the kind of thing we study. They are the respiration of the ocean, a breathing in and out. It's rhythmic. Still, people are always screwing up on predicting the tides. Sure, they get high tides plus or minus the minutes and plus or minus a foot or so—but not exactly. The world authority on tides—Fergus Wood—listed 136 representative cycles in the Sun-Moon system that have a bearing on tides. And then you have to bring in other factors like the shoreline. Where I'm living at Laguna Beach the tide is different than at Newport Beach six miles away.

In an effort to describe the study of cycles, Gertrude Shirk wrote:

> We can say that the Foundation for the Study of Cycles looks for evidence of regularity in the ups and downs in those figures (where we have regularity we have predictability); it tries to find out in which cases the regular ups and downs have meaning; and in which cases they are just the result of chance; it tries to find the causes that could create such behavior if it is not the result of chance. The particular kind of figures which we study are called *time series*. Time series are just figures that are written down for successive periods of time. Continuous daily temperature readings make a time series. The average monthly sunspot record makes a

time series. A cycle is the characteristic of a time series to get back to where it was before. In our definition, we used the term "regularity in the ups and downs." That is we look for rhythmic cycles, figures that tend to get back to where they were before with some degree of rhythm, with a sort of beat.

Shirk's successor as research director, Richard Mogey, who would become the Foundation's executive director, elaborated on her definition:

A cycle has to repeat the data a certain number of times before being considered a true cycle. A bare minimum is five times, but I think that's too low. I prefer at least ten times. I like to go back into the 1600s and 1700s when I can. I know it will get out of sync, and I want to see what it does when that happens. I want it to get back into the same beat, to pick up the beat that it left behind. Even when a cycle gets off, it should return to its original phasing. For instance, the forty-month cycle that Dewey and Shirk worked on so long has been out of phase occasionally but when it comes back it is right back where it should be.

Cycles are easier to identify—or, at least, to substantiate—when hard data, such as records of the stock market or the time series cited by Shirk, are available. But believers in cycles are convinced that they can be seen in processes that are more difficult to reduce to numbers. One of America's leading geographers, the late Ellsworth Huntington of Yale University, defined cycles in the broadest terms in his masterwork, *Mainsprings of Civilization*:

The whole history of life is a record of cycles. In the vast geological periods plants and animals of one great order after another rose to importance, flourished, and declined. In prehistoric times successive species of manlike creatures passed across the stage. In the historic period nations have risen and fallen; types of civilization have grown great and decayed; science, art, and literature have been full of vigor and originality only to fall into deadly weakness and conventionalism. In modern business few things are more disturbing than the cycles which seem to become more extreme as time goes on. In each of these examples, some form of existence or type of activity starts a certain condition, goes through a series of changes, and comes back to essentially the same condition as at the beginning. An explosion, for example, sets still air in violent motion. There is a loud sound and buildings fall. Then the whole thing dies down. The air may be full of smoke and dust, but so far as motion is concerned, it has returned to its old condition of stillness. The life cycle of plants and animals also illustrates the matter. It starts with nonexistence, passes through many stages, and ends once more with non-existence.

Despite the wide angle of his lens, Huntington claimed that he could see the same characteristics that Dewey, Shirk, and Mogey described. Some aspect of "coming around to the place of beginning" is basic to a definition of a cycle, but there are other factors that must be taken into consideration according to Huntington. One of these is repetition, which Huntington illustrated with reproduction. A plant, a person, or a nation can go through a life cycle and disappear without leaving a successor. But if a plant produces seeds that take root, a new life cycle arises from the old, and this can go on indefinitely. Thus there are both individual cycles and reproductive cycles. Another factor is regularity, or rhythm. An explosion might create a cycle in the air, but there would be no rhythm involved unless a similar explosion occurred at regular intervals. Akin to rhythm but more precise is "periodicity," about which Huntington wrote:

> By this we mean a regular recurrence at specified and hence predictable intervals. The day with its phases of light and darkness is of this kind. So are the seasons and tides. Many people are beginning to suspect that definite periodicity goes much farther than this. They think that it is found in cycles of business and even in the rise and fall of types of civilization and the long eras of geology. The definite periodicity is supposed to have its origin in purely physical conditions which repeat themselves as regularly as the motions of the planets or the waves of different length which constitute heat, light, and electricity. Such physical cycles are superimposed upon one another in bewildering profusion. The length of some is only a fraction of a second and that of others millions of years. When the effects of all these periodic cycles are added to those of rhythmic but not periodic cycles, the result is bound to be highly complex. For that reason many events which are really due to the combined effect of many periodic causes are commonly supposed to be hopelessly irregular and unpredictable.

Among those who shared Huntington's belief that there are some cycles that do not arise from mathematical analysis alone was the late historian and sometime presidential adviser Arthur M. Schlesinger, Jr. His book *The Cycles of American History* elaborates a thesis put forward by his father, also a historian, seventy years ago. A surprising proponent of cycles is Lee Iacocca, the former head of Chrysler, who offered a rather jaunty definition of cycles in his book *Talking Straight*: "Life is full of all sorts of cycles. Some of them are predictable—night follows day; fall follows summer; tides follow the Moon. Those are the ones God takes care of. Then there are the ones people take care of: business cycles, energy cycles, automotive cycles. Those we manage to screw up good."

The French have a saying, *plus ca change, plus c'est la meme chose;* or the more things change, the more they stay the same. This seems to be one possible definition of the cycle. But it does not fit any better than a perfect circle or a sine wave. Cycles or no, things do change. This is one reason for skepticism in regard to cycles. A case in point is the stock market, for which hard data for statistical analysis is available. If cycle proponents crowed about foreshadowing the 1987 crash and connected it with historic downs, such as 1929, their critics countered with, "How can you talk about cycles when nothing's really the same this time? For instance, the low was around 384 in 1929 and only 1616 in 1987. . . ." Harvey Wasserman, who sees cyclic rhythms in the softer data of history, came up with a visual image that neatly solves the paradox of change within sameness. For his book *American Born and Reborn* he drew a spiral rising in ever tightening circles to accommodate the so-called progress and perceived acceleration in human events that make today's America different from that of the colonial era, yet still cyclical in character. The spiral analogy—I personally see it as a spiral staircase—can also accommodate natural history with its evidence of evolution. The spiral makes so much sense to me as a layman that I tried it out on the professional staff of the Foundation for the Study of Cycles and found the members largely in agreement. Mogey's telling comment on the paradox is that a cycle results in repetition but not duplication.

There is yet another aspect of the cycle that makes it harder to define than the rose—its individuality. Every rose is just another rose, but as Mogey said, "Cycles are idealized. They're a little like Platonic ideas. Plato used to say that there is an idea of man but no man is like that idea. Uniqueness is more significant than similarity in the way a man develops. In a cycle you have an ideal rhythm, but the unique way in which a cycle works out its uniqueness is much more critical." This was Mogey's comment on market cycles. In *Cycles of Becoming* Alexander Ruperti writes of cycles in human affairs:

> If a cycle is reduced to a closed circle of repetitive events, it cannot have the creative, evolutionary meaning it possesses when understood to be the expression of a creative process. And yet, as a matter of fact, both interpretations of a cycle are correct. The *structure* of a cycle in time, i.e., its duration, repeats itself. A day cycle repeats itself every twenty-four hours; the lunation cycle, on which the month is based, repeats itself at each new moon; the year cycle repeats itself every twelve months. But those who limit their understanding of the significance of a cycle to such a repetitive sequence of time values—days, months, or years—forget that what *happens* during a given day, month or year, does *not* repeat itself exactly. The way we act and the meaning we find in a particular experience during a given cycle represent the creative, individual element.

The fact that the cycle does not lend itself to simplistic definition is one reason why it might be the clue to solving many mysteries of the universe. However cycles may be seen or described, their presence and influence has been felt throughout all of recorded history. Using the standard image, Ralph Waldo Emerson, the sage of Concord, expressed this thought in words that rival those of Shakespeare or Stein: "The eye is the first circle; the horizon which it forms is the second, and throughout nature this primary figure is repeated without end. It is the highest emblem in the cipher of the world."

CHAPTER 2

A New Science in the Making

"Basically, we are hammering out a new science," Edward R. Dewey, founder of the Foundation for the Study of Cycles, told *New Yorker* writer John Brooks in 1962. "If it is accepted, it must receive the support and endorsement of natural as well as social sciences." Although Dewey skillfully wielded his hammer, his work has yet to be recognized as a separate field of academic study such as biology or economics. The holistic nature of cycle thinking has resulted in the discovery of hundreds of cycles across a wide spectrum of both the natural and social sciences: sunspots and solar phenomena in astronomy; electrical potential of trees in botany; pigment changes in salamanders in herpetology; air movements and wind direction in climatology; emotions and mental activity in medicine; activity of electrons and molecular vibrations in physics; advertising efficiency in economics; and civil and international war battles in sociology.

However broad, Dewey's study of cycles fits several different definitions of *science* in *Webster's*, the best being "knowledge covering general truths or the operation of general laws, especially as obtained and tested through scientific method." Dewey believed there was "something out there" driving cycles, and his aim was to find out what it could be through the scientific method. To this end, he heeded theoretical physicist Richard P. Feynman's advice: "In regard to cycles, the proper scientific assumption to start with is that they are chance. If they cannot reasonably be chance, the next assumption should be that they are caused within the phenomenon or the system of which the phenomenon is an interacting part. Only if the cycles cannot be the result of chance or endogenous causes should we undertake to postulate external and or exogenous causes." How and why he would proceed to eliminate chance and endogenous causes in the many cycles under study was set forth by Dewey in an article called "The Case for Cycles," published in *Cycles* in July, 1967. The introduction of this article is worth quoting:

> There is considerable evidence . . . that there are natural environmental forces that alternately stimulate and depress mankind in the mass. These same forces may also affect plant and animal life, weather, and even such normally unchanging things as chemical reactions. . . . The argument for the existence of these forces runs something like this: Almost everything fluctuates. Many things fluctuate in cycles or waves. Many of these waves are spaced regularly and have other characteristics that indicate that the spacing cannot reasonably be chance. Nonchance spacing must, by the meaning of the words, have a cause. This cause must be internal (dynamic) or interacting (feedback or predator-prey) or external. . . .
>
> Let us admit straightaway, however, that in spite of the evidence, the case for the existence of such forces has not been proved.

We do not know that forces of this sort surround us. If they exist, no one knows what they are—although there are some guesses. No one has ever seen them—they are as invisible as radio waves. Few people have even imagined them. We merely assume them, working backward from observed behavior. . . . Radios and radio waves provide a good analogy. We are all familiar with radios and know in a general way how they operate. Each radio sending station emits waves of a different number of cycles per second. The radio receivers in our houses respond to one or another of these vibrations, according to where we set our tuning dial.

Now imagine that a man from Mars is in my home for a visit. He is a good physicist, but he knows nothing of radio sending stations. He studies my radio. From this study he determines that, when he sets the dial a certain way, the radio vibrates 79.4 thousand times a second; and that when my second radio is set to vibrate this way also, it plays the same tune. With these facts before him it does not take him very long to postulate that both rooms are filled with invisible vibrations of some sort to which both radios respond, and that somewhere there is something that generates these vibrations.

Further, as the same thing happens when he sets the dials at 104.2, he deduces that there is a second generating force—and so on for each setting.

Up to this point the existence of these waves or these sending stations is purely presumptive. He deduces them by logical reasoning.

Suppose our man from Mars now comes across statistics or studies which show that every ten years or so rabbits in Canada are more abundant, thus creating a rhythmic cycle of great regularity; the population increasing for four to five years and then decreasing for an equal span of time. He also discovers that rainfall in London and rainfall in India fluctuate in cycles of the same length. So does the abundance of ozone at Paris, the number of caterpillars in New Jersey, the abundance of salmon on both sides of the Atlantic, as well as many other things. What's more, he finds all things having cycles of this same length tend to crest at the same time.

He also reads that other things act as if they respond to cyclic forces of other time intervals and that always, cycles of the same length tend to synchronize.

"Why!" he says. "It's just like that radio thing that I looked at first, except that these phenomena are the receiving sets instead of those little black boxes; and the environmental forces that I deduce are thousands and thousands of times longer. These cycles are measured in years instead of fractions of a second.

"Now," he adds, "I'll ask my host to explain all this to me. He can tell me, I'm sure, what makes the boxes play the same tunes when set to the same frequency, what makes dozens of phenomena fluctuate together as if they were subject to environmental forces."

Our friend from Mars overrates me. I can explain a little about the radio waves and sending stations, but as for the longer cycles, I am lost. All I can do is share his belief that there must be something that causes them.

Now I am going to ask you to make an effort of credulity and admit—just for the sake of getting on with the story—that these behaviors are so, and that they are the result of some external, invisible, and as yet unknown forces. . . . I wish you merely to consider the implications and corollaries if this thesis proves to be correct.

The first implication is that law, regularity, order, and pattern exist in vast areas hitherto thought to be patternless. A discovery of this sort is akin to the discovery by the ancients that the planets (so called from the Greek word planet, meaning wanderer) indeed have regular and predictable movements. It is akin to the discovery that the fluctuating levels of the sea (the tides) are regular and hence predictable. It is akin to the discovery of germs, radiation, X-rays, or atoms. It is akin to the discovery that the atomic weights of the elements can be arranged into a periodic table. In fact, it is similar to any of the great discoveries since the dawn of civilization that have driven caprice, disorder, and chaos back toward limbo. I can think of nothing that will extend the area of order into more different areas, more different disciplines, more different phenomena than cycle study—if these postulated forces really exist.

The second implication of cycle study is the enormous increase in the area of predictability. It is the business of science to predict. Thus, two atoms of hydrogen and one atom of oxygen (H_2O) under certain conditions will always combine to produce one molecule of water. Insofar as cycles are nonchance phenomena and continue after discovery, we have notably and importantly increased this particular function of science. A way has been opened up to mankind not only to forecast, but thus to circumvent many aspects of what hitherto has seemed the capriciousness of fate.

Third, insofar as cycles are meaningful, all science that has been developed in the absence of cycle knowledge is inadequate and partial. Thus, if cyclic forces are real, any theory of economics, or sociology, or history, or medicine, or climatology that ignores nonchance rhythms is manifestly incomplete, as medicine was before the discovery of germs.

Fourth, if these cyclic forces are real, there is a much greater degree of interrelationship within nature than was previously realized, since the same cycles appear in many different natural and social sciences. The implications are one of wholeness instead of emphasis we so often see upon smaller and smaller sections of knowledge.

Fifth, if these forces exist, man is further deflated. When a knowledge of cycles becomes widespread, it will create a jolt to man's ego similar to that created by the knowledge that many of his actions are dictated by his subconscious; that the Earth is not the center of the universe; that even our galaxy is but a speck of dust. To a much greater extent then formerly realized, man has been a cork on the tides of destiny. However, knowledge of these forces—when we know that they really exist—will enable man to foil them. Sufficient knowledge always has this effect.

Sixth, all in all, the Universe is shown to be an even more marvelous place than has hitherto been realized.

Although the answer to what the "something out there" was eluded Dewey, he plodded on in what he considered the pursuit of science. His son, Edward S. Dewey, told me Dewey was "a workaholic—no golf, no tennis, no dancing, no drinking." He was an overachiever who was equally demanding of his associates, according to Gertrude Shirk, who recalled, "He couldn't understand people who would take an hour for a lunch they could eat in twenty minutes." But Shirk found him to be "an interesting man, more or less a man of the world" with whom she had never ending discussions about their mutual interest in their field of study. Despite his fierce dedication to the cause of cycles, Dewey retained an open mind into his eighties. Dewey was slowing down physically, but up to the week he died he was full of ideas," Shirk told me:

> For example, we had an astronomer on staff—a Ph.D. candidate in astronomy. He pointed out that if you want to make a comparison between timing in planets and timing on Earth, you have to be aware of the fact that planets do not move at a constant speed. So Dewey said, "Give me the varying speeds of the planets so that I will know when they are going faster and slower." He was working with a 5.9-year cycle in cotton prices and a 5.9-year

astronomical cycle. What he was looking for was to see whether, if an anomaly developed in cotton prices, a counterpart anomaly occurred in astronomy.

Dewey did not have time to finish this project: He died in 1978, only nine years after making his case for cycles, and he was full of confidence in the future of his science. According to his son, Edward S. Dewey, "He was very pleased with what he had done with his life. Toward the end he was getting some recognition. He was, for instance, one of the few American members of the World Academy of Arts and Sciences. He was very happy, and he went out like a rocket. He visualized himself as the man before Copernicus—that is, after he had finished all the work he had to do, the next man would come along in twenty or so years and tie up all the knots."

The knots are still not tied as of this writing. Indeed, in keeping with scientific endeavor they may never be. But Dewey's confidence that cycles would take an appropriate place in the scientific world was well placed. As cycles turn up in every new discovery of physics, their existence cannot much longer be ignored in academic circles. Meanwhile, the study of cycles is a continuing concern of scientists from a variety of backgrounds and disciplines. Because of the holistic and unorthodox nature of cycle study, it has attracted mostly independent thinkers. One of these is New Zealander Ray Tomes, who came up with the staggering equations that form the scientific underpinning of his theory of heavenly harmonics.

"I led a very lonely path initially in cycles," he wrote me:

Once I found out about Dewey and the Foundation for the Study of Cycles, I discovered that much of what I had worked out myself over many years had already been found by others.

And such things as the cosmic origin of cycles was one of these . . . [discovered by] Belarusan Alexander Chizhevsky, once one of the presidents of the International Congress of Biophysics, and Dewey (the two most thorough cycles researchers) eventually coming to that conclusion. People who were ridiculed for finding cycles were eventually proved right by space observations, e.g. Nicholas Abbott, the University of Wisconsin chemical engineer who found cycles in solar output from ground base observations—after all, they called the solar output "the solar constant," and now satellite measurements have confirmed all he said. I think there is a thorough blindness to the truth of the workings of our universe in academic circles even more than the general public. At least in the public there are people open to these ideas even if they are mostly not rigorous. We need openness and rigor to get to the truth.

It would be hard to find more rigor than that shown by Fergus J. Wood, trained in astronomy but famed as an authority on tides. On the question of whether the study of cycles is scientific, Wood wanted to make it crystal clear that his discovery of the role cyclical configurations of celestial bodies play in extremely high or low tides is based on the most painstaking and systematic study.

"We have established for the first time that there are definite astronomical cycles," he told me:

We call them luni-solar cycles, a combination of the moon's action and the sun's action. Because they do exist in nature, we've been able to do what we've done in terms of putting down when these things will happen and what they will do.

I made a large number of tests of this sort of thing because in science we cannot be content on the basis of one particular circumstance. I did this for 100 events or more. We not only take many events, but we twist them around to try to show that they're wrong so that we know they are right if they work out. One test is to take something that is absolutely devoid of any meaning in terms of what it is that you are doing and use that as a parameter on which to base the systematic work that you are doing.

An example is that I took five different coastal towns of the same name throughout the world. The selection had nothing whatever to do with the physical law that I was exploring. If you take five remote places joined only by the circumstances of name and the hypothesis still works out, you believe you are on the right track.

I took five towns with the name of Newport—Newport, Oregon; Newport Beach, California; Newport News, Virginia; and two Newports in England on different coasts. I took tidal flow at those places all the way back in time—in some cases to A.D. 1099. I associated them only through mathematical luni-solar relationships. The numerical value is determined by what the Moon and Sun are doing at the time, and simple multiples of these values will work out to the distance and time between events. In this case, the celestial circumstances that should have produced coastal flooding did produce coastal flooding in the Newports throughout history.

A different type of scientist in cycles is John P. Bagby. His research on earthquakes is as detailed and disciplined as Wood's and his range of interests was as interdisciplinary as the study of cycles. A mechanical engineer at Hughes Aircraft in Los Angeles, what Bagby remembers most from his education was a professor who told him that once a person is trained in one subject, he can train himself in others. Bagby did this with the enthusiastic help and encouragement of his scientifically-minded wife, Loretta. Trained as a medical technician, Loretta Bagby pursued further study in medicine and chemistry. While rearing three children, she collaborated with her husband on studies and experiments in astronomy and physics that shook one of the pillars of modern scientific thought—the law of gravity.

The law of gravity was established more than 300 years ago as the result of discoveries by Galileo Galilei and Sir Isaac Newton. Galileo "proved" that the acceleration of any falling body is constant and has the same value for all bodies. Newton "proved" that any two bodies in the universe attract each other in proportion to the product of their masses and inversely to the square of their distances from each other. The law of gravity has been foundational to the study of science and engineering, but increasingly such inquiring minds as the Bagbys' have questioned the assumption that gravity is the uniformly steady force described by Galileo and Newton. Because of anomalies in gravity's action, there is even talk of a fifth or sixth force in addition to the four forces supposedly holding the universe together—gravity, electromagnetism, and the so-called strong and weak forces binding atomic nuclei.

The Bagbys' temerity in challenging an iron rule of a science is of interest in regards to how we define a science. Their story begins in the 1950s when John Bagby sought work at Bell & Howell, an Illinois camera maker. "They said my work had all been with large mechanisms and pipes and forgings and castings—a forty-inch pipe isn't a camera," he recalled, "and I said, 'Well, an engineer is an engineer, and I should be able to work with small things, too.'" Although he was hired, Bagby soon discovered that he would have to work outside the system. Discouraged by the company's engineering department when he came up with an idea for an automatic focus mechanism for cameras, he and Loretta worked together on it at home, assembling experimental models on the kitchen table. Evidently operating on what Bagby called the "NIH factor—Not Invented Here," the engineering vice president rejected Bagby's request to put the camera into development at the company.

In retrospect, this became an important turning point in Bagby's development as an experimental scientist. In talking to me, he credited Loretta with giving him the heart to pursue these interests outside of his regular job. "Her thought was that, if you are afraid to make mistakes, you will never take risks," he says. "She encouraged me to take more risks than they were allowing. When the vice president of engineering and the chief engineer went on vacation, I took the camera to a business manager named Bill Roberts who immediately arranged funding for the experiment. The result wasn't all pleasant. I didn't get a raise for two and a half years, wasn't promoted, was taken out of my job, and in general was really roughed up. But we got the camera."

By the time I talked to him, Bagby shared eight patents on solar-powered automatic focus cameras and had developed a much thicker skin with respect to rejection by orthodox thinkers—a rejection that wasn't limited to the industrial world. Possibly because he was writing about subjects for which he had no standard career credentials, it took Bagby thirteen years and innumerable revisions before his first scientific paper was finally published in the journal *Nature*. But the persistence that enabled Bagby to get published at all was an essential ingredient of the Bagbys' investigation into the law of gravity. For a long time, Bagby had wondered whether it was really true that bodies of different weight and composition fell at the same velocity and whether bodies weighed the same at different times. He and Loretta concocted an experiment in which they weighed objects on a balance and observed how their weights changed relative to each other over a span of time. It was tedious and meticulous work. When John Bagby left Illinois for a job in California in 1978, Loretta stayed behind to keep the children in school and sell their home. It turned out to be a separation of fourteen months during which each filled the lonely hours by conducting experiments that they discussed by phone. Using one empty weekend for intensive work, Bagby set an alarm to wake himself every twenty minutes over a period of forty-eight hours in order to measure bits of lead, brass, copper, aluminum, water, and ice on a scale. As a result of such efforts, the Bagbys decided that there were more variations in weights than allowable under Newton's law and that they were cyclical in character.

"We couldn't make sense of it at first. Sometimes we saw a force that was positive and sometimes a force that was negative and sometimes none at all," he told me. "Then suddenly we saw a pattern. It was irregular but cyclic, periodic. We analyzed it and found that there were two main cycles involved— at two point sixty-six and four hours." Convinced that there was an outside, cyclical force involved in recurrent weight changes in the same object, the Bagbys reasoned that, as he explained to Shari Roan of the *Orange County Register*, "The moon or stars or planets were acting in gravitational enhancement. We felt it was due to their alignment. We were convinced that the law of gravity was wrong. How could something be the same and change in weight? We were frightened. I thought these were sacred laws, but I couldn't accept them."

Attempting to interest others in these insights was as frustrating as attempting to sell the concept of an automatic focus camera, and, until 1986 the Bagbys turned to studies of the relationship between celestial gravitational forces and earthquakes. In that year, a physicist with the proper academic credentials—Ephraim Fischbach of Purdue University—joined the challengers of the law of gravity by announcing that all bodies do not fall at the same rate and postulating that the attraction between two bodies had as much to do with their chemical composition as with their mass alone. Hearing this, the Bagbys went back into battle against the impregnable scientific citadel of gravity. In the two-story foyer of their home in Anaheim, they loaded one paper cup with wood and another with pennies of equal weight, dropped them simultaneously from a height of eight feet and filmed the descent with a camcorder. The cups interchanged positions like runners on a race track with one gaining as much as one-and-a-half inches on the other and falling back again, and they didn't always land at the same time. This happened in cyclical patterns in repeated experiments.

In another experiment, Bagby constructed a horizontal balsa wood pendulum and put equally weighted but different sized disks of silicon and molybdenum at either end. Setting the pendulum to swing horizontally, Bagby took the elapsed time of eight swings divided by eight to get an average and repeated the experiment eight more times; then repeated the experiment at twenty minute intervals; then changed the disks to opposite ends of the pendulum and went through the entire experience once more; then rotated the balance 180 degrees and repeated the experiment for a third time. The upshot? More cyclical patterns that suggest an outside force in the form of gravitational waves from the planets.

It was 1987 before Bagby heard of the Foundation for the Study of Cycles, located almost in his own backyard at Irvine. He attended a spring symposium staged by the Foundation and found himself among like-minded mavericks in the sciences. "I learned that other people have worked in other fields with a lot of the same abuse as we've had, but they all have the same bias that we do—that there is this influence from the planets," he said. But Bagby was under no illusion that his postulations would find their way into the scientific mainstream any faster than those of Dewey or, for that matter, Newton, whose ideas were in circulation for twenty years before they brought about a scientific revolution.

The synchrony in timing between celestial and terrestrial cycles, or between cycles in unrelated phenomena on Earth, was one of the findings of the Foundation that caused Dewey to lay claim to the name of science. "We began to look more closely at all the cycles with the same length, and what we discovered convinced not only me but a large body of previously doubting scientists that cycles are a reality," he wrote in his book *Cycles*. "We discovered that all cycles of the same length tend to turn at the same time! Now if it is difficult to find cycles with identical lengths in unrelated phenomena by chance alone, think how much more difficult it is to find cycles with identical lengths that also turn at or about the same calendar time. What amazed us even more was to learn that all cycles of the same length behave in the same way. This was unusually powerful evidence that we were dealing with real and not random behavior." Dewey's evidence that there is a synchrony in cycles is impressive, and the association of phenomena through these cycles is fascinating. Here are a few samples:

- Among some 37 cycles of 9.6 or 9.7 years in length are those of colored fox abundance in Canada, salmon abundance in England, tent caterpillar abundance in New Jersey, ozone content of the atmosphere in London and Paris, heart disease in New England, and international battles in wars.
- Among 10 cycles turning every 5.91 years are business failures since 1857, combined stock prices since 1871, grouse abundance since 1848, and sunspots since 1749.
- Among 12 cycles with an 18.2-year period are marriages in the United States, real estate activity since 1851, flood stages of the Nile River since 641, and Java tree rings since 1514.

Dewey admitted that the reason for the interrelation of certain cycles remained a mystery, but he was sure that there was a reason to be found. The strength of his conviction emerges from Gertrude Shirk's story about the puzzle he was trying to solve in the last weeks of his life. Although he remained appropriately cautious and tentative in public statements, Dewey was evidently quite certain as to where his science was leading. "Toward the end my father felt very sure that he had put it together—in other words, the cause was extraterrestrial in some way, " Edward S. Dewey said. "He talked about such things as latitudinal variations in the abundance of animals that could be accounted for only by extraterrestrial forces—forces such as gravity and the relations of the planets. He used magnetic force as the kind of force that could affect us en masse." It's not hard to imagine the excitement that Dewey would have felt in learning of the work of scientists like Wood and Bagby, and he would surely have kept a sharp eye on research that was reported in the book *The Body Electric: Electromagnetism and the Foundation of Life* by Robert O. Becker, M.D., and Gary Selden. This book contains a section with a bearing on Dewey's search because it suggests a mechanism for linking cycles:

> At the end of the nineteenth century, geophysicists found that the earth's magnetic field varied as the moon revolved around it. In the same period, anthropologists were learning that most preliterate cultures reckoned their calendar time primarily by the moon. These discoveries led Svante Arrhenius, the Swedish natural philosopher and father of ion chemistry, to suggest that his tidal magnetic rhythm was an innate timekeeper regulating the few obvious biocycles then known.
>
> Since then we've learned of many other cyclic changes in the energy structure around us:
>
> - The Earth's electromagnetic field is largely a result of interaction between the magnetic field per se, emanating from the planet's molten iron-nickel core, and the charged gas of the ionosphere. It varies with the lunar day and month, and there's also a yearly change as we revolve around the Sun.
> - A cycle of several centuries is driven from somewhere in the galactic center.
> - The Earth's surface and the ionosphere form an electrodynamic resonating cavity that produces micropulsations in the magnetic field at extremely low frequencies, from about twenty-five per second down to one every ten seconds. Most of the

micropulsation energy is concentrated at about ten hertz per second.

- Solar flares spew charged particles into the Earth's field, causing magnetic storms. The particles join those already in the outer reaches of the field (the Van Allen belts), which protect us by absorbing these and other high-energy rays.

- Every flash of lightning releases a burst of radio energy at kilocycle frequencies, which travels parallel to the magnetic field's lines of force and bounces back and forth between the north and south poles many times before fading out.

- The surface and ionosphere act as the charged plates of a condenser (a charge storage device), producing an electrostatic field of hundreds of thousands of volts per foot. This electric field continually ionizes many of the molecules of the air's gases, and it, too, pulses in the ELF (extremely low frequency) range.

- There are also large direct currents continually flowing within the ionosphere and as telluric (within-the-earth) currents, generating their own subsidiary electromagnetic fields.

- In the 1970s we learned that the Sun's magnetic field is divided from pole to pole into sectors, like the sections of an orange, and the field in each sector is oriented in the direction opposite to adjacent sectors. About every eight days the Sun's rotation brings a new region of the interplanetary (solar) magnetic field opposite us, and the Earth's field is slightly changed in response to the flip-flop in polarity. The sector boundary's passage also induces a day or two of turbulence.

The potential interactions among all these electromagnetic phenomena and life are almost infinitely complex.

That there are such interactions is proved by the many animal and human experiments the authors cite. One of the most convincing involved hundreds of volunteers who spent several months in bunkers that isolated them from any sense of time. One group was not shielded from electromagnetic fields; the other was. "Persons in both rooms soon developed irregular rhythms," Dr. Becker reported, "but those in the completely shielded room had significantly longer ones. Those still exposed to the Earth's field kept to a rhythm close to twenty-four hours. In some of these people, a few variables wandered from the circadian rate, but they always stabilized at some new rate harmony with the basic one—two days instead of one, for example. People kept from contact with the Earth's field, on the other hand, became thoroughly desynchronized." When a very weak electric fields (0.025 volts per centimeter) pulsing at ten hertz was reintroduced into the shielded bunker, a normal cycle returned to most of the subjects' biological rhythms.

Dewey anticipated the development that research which is scientific by any definition would continue to reveal the cyclical nature of the universe. According to his son, "for him, the intellectual ballgame was over. He didn't worry about when other people would catch up to him." In his eighties as this book was written, Edward S. Dewey did express concern that scientific proof of his father's postulation was yet to come, and he hoped to see it within his lifetime. The possibility that his wish may be gratified was greatly enhanced when David Michael Perales resurrected the Foundation for the Study of Cycles on May 2, 2005.

Although comfortably headquartered in Albuquerque, New Mexico, the Foundation maintains the records and traditions of Dewey's time. Its mission statement resonates with the founder's own: "Our mission is to discover, understand, and explain the true nature and origin of cycles, thereby solving the mystery of recurrent rhythmic phenomena, as has been observed in both the natural and social sciences, and while so doing, to instruct others, and to apply this new knowledge for the greater good of all life." In carrying out this mission, the Foundation has been greatly enhanced by the use of the Internet, through which its knowledge and services have been made available to anyone with a computer.

Under the guidance of President Perales, the Foundation has achieved remarkable growth in less than four years. It has 4,000 active members and an e-mail list of 38,000.

Among the countries with a working relationship to the Foundation are New Zealand, Australia, Netherlands, Sweden, Panama, Thailand, Hong Kong, Germany, Denmark, and Egypt.

A discovery by David Perales resonates with Dewey's idea of a coming Copernicus. Perales worked as a sales representative for Encyclopedia Britannica and liked to relax by walking on the beach and plotting movements of the heavenly bodies that fascinated him. He spent years when away from his job in sales to pursue his astronomical searches. The rest of the story is best told in excerpts from two letters by Richard Mogey, former director of the "old" Foundation who came out of retirement to serve as a director and head of research for the "new" one. The resonance is in the date of Mogey's first letter—May 23, 1997, well within Dewey's prediction at the time of his death in 1978 that a successor would appear in "twenty years or so" to complete his search for the celestial driver of earthly cycles. "Over six years ago," Mogey wrote in his 1997 letter:

David Perales called me on the phone and asked to make an appointment to discuss some research that he was working on. The next week he left Louisiana and arrived in my office in Southern California. He showed me some unique market timing discoveries that he had made. I frequently am presented with all kinds of systems and ideas, but David's was different. I was profoundly impressed with both the theory and potential application of this new way of viewing market dynamics. I urged him to computerize these findings and that began a six-year-long collaboration. I have also taken an active part in helping him with the programming and therefore have an intimate knowledge of the principles of the timing system. I remain impressed. Since I have absolutely no financial interest in his work, I have remained an independent observer. I have personally seen the historical accuracy of his timing tools as well as watched it work in the future for more than ten months. David is an excellent researcher and has great integrity.

On February 3, 2009, Richard Mogey wrote another letter:

I have been studying cycles since 1966, almost as long as Edward R. Dewey. In that time I have done studies for corporations, and as research director at the Foundation, some of my early researches for corporations was to statistically analyze planetary cycles in relation to the future and equity markets. . . .

When I met David Perales in 1991 at the Foundation's offices in Irvine everything I had studied to that point changed. His work is truly revolutionary, and with it he has transformed the dry, untenable statistics into a dynamic, real-time understanding of how human beings and capital come together. His independent research is the seed of an immense potential for profitable trading systems, when melded with cycles work. This work which has been held close to the vest for so many years is now for the first time to be made available to researchers through a new module in Techsignal, called Planetary Data Module, or PDM.

It would appear that a new science is already in place, and the hammering can stop. In the light of their stories, it is clear that the researchers associated with cycle study display the imagination, diligence and patience that constitute the definition of scientific method in any dictionary. It is also apparent that, using this method, Perales and Mogey see a "something out there" with a harmonic in human activity, as predicted by Dewey nearly half a century ago. In the chaotic times of this writing, it is comforting to note the birth of a new science that postulates a universe of order and predictability.

CHAPTER 3

FOLLOW THE MONEY

During the advent of the latest recession, sharp-eyed cycle students throughout the world got a priceless gift. Executives of the Foundation for the Study of Cycles published warnings in the summer of 2008 of financial disasters to come—time enough for timid followers to get out of the way and bold ones to turn a profit. Although using knowledge of cycles to protect or increase one's wealth is not the only benefit of studying cycles, it is historically the best known and most tangible employment of such study.

The Rothschild financial dynasty is credited by cycle scholars with discovering the monetary value of this predictive device in the nineteenth century. The Rothschilds did not look upon cycles as a science but as a business secret that improved performance in their investment enterprises, and they guarded it as closely as manufacturers do their inventions. The study of cycles did not come into general business use until the stock market crash and subsequent Great Depression prompted businessmen and economists to look for new answers to their problems.

These events led directly to the establishment of the Foundation for the Study of Cycles. But in the beginning even the Foundation followed the Rothschild rule of secrecy in order to raise money by selling cycle analysis to corporations. Fortunately for the existence of the Foundation, there has continued to be enough business interest even in shared secrets to demonstrate to the general public that cycles are taken quite seriously by presumably hardheaded people of commerce.

This was not always so. Dewey, a man who was able to view his obsession with a healthy sense of humor, liked to recount two tales of his early efforts to interest businesspeople in what an awareness of cycles could do for them. A man he called Charlie, vice president of one of the nation's ten top corporations, listened to Dewey with interest and then said, "I think you really have something, but I don't want to get in bad around here."

Charlie called the company's comptroller into his office and asked, "Bill, how much can I spend for a crazy idea and be able to laugh it off if anything ever comes up about it?"

"$500," Bill replied.

"That's what I thought, too," Charlie said and turned to Dewey. "All right, Mr. Dewey, make a study for us of the cycles in our industry. Hold the cost to $500 and send the study and bill to me."

Dewey carried through, got the $500 but no follow-up. In another case, the vice president of a New York bank also seemed interested but finally said, "I believe in astrology. I never take any action without consulting my astrologer. When were you born?"

When Dewey gave him the date, the man said, "I'll send this date on to my astrologer. If he approves, I'll contact you further."

Dewey never heard from the man, which may account for the fact that the Foundation did not consider astrology, as popularly publicized and practiced, a proper part of the science of cycles.

One of the most enthusiastic and longest serving chairmen of the Foundation was W. Clement Stone, a millionaire Chicago entrepreneur, whose support for the Foundation was in gratitude of the making of his millions. He told the story of his personal involvement in his publication *Success: The Magazine for Achievers*:

> Many years ago, I had a large loan at the American National Bank and Trust Company in Chicago. One day, Paul Raymond, vice president in charge of loans, telephoned me and said, "Clem, I am sending a book to everyone who has a large loan with us." I laughed and responded, "I can read. What's the name of the book?" He said, "*Cycles* by Edward R. Dewey and Edwin F. Dakin."
>
> Because I had developed the habit at an early age to recognize, relate, assimilate, and apply principles from what I read, saw, heard, thought, and experienced, I discovered a missing ingredient on how to predict my future and make a fortune—not lose it. When I see my business leveling off, I use a principle learned from *Cycles*: Start a new trend with a new life, new blood, new ideas, new activities. That's why I now predict that I shall increase my wealth by a few hundred million dollars in the next five years.

You, too, can predict your future and make a fortune if you are willing to study, learn and apply the principles of cycles and trends and daily engage in creative, positive thinking time.

Peter Borish, former chairman of the Foundation for the Study of Cycles, entered cycleland in a manner very much like that of Stone. In 1985, after a stint at the New York Federal Reserve Bank, he joined Tudor Investments in New York where, as he put it, "My first marching orders were to learn as much as I could about cycles and seasonality, because we felt that if the market, whichever market you are looking at, behaves in a cyclic manner, it should be relatively fixed in terms of periodicity." A study of the data over a 220-year period has, for example, established an approximately seventeen and three quarter year cycle in cotton prices; a study begun in 1860 has fixed a three and a half year cycle in corn prices. In each case, the peaks were approximately eighteen and three-and-a-half-years apart, respectively, on average. Borish's research into cycles was not only convincing enough to lead him into active participation in the Foundation but to widen his view of its function. "My idea is to make the Foundation an interdisciplinary medium for exchange of information on all cycles, not just in the market," he told me.

Like the board and membership, most of the staff in Borish's time came out of the business world, including Richard Mogey, former executive director, and his former managing director, Gary Bosley, both of whom learned to use cycles in the markets. The Foundation's first research director, Gertrude Shirk, a pioneer in both cycle analysis and careers for women, graduated with a degree in business administration from the University of Pittsburgh and went to work in the department of economic and statistical analysis at Westinghouse Electric Corporation. In a foreshadowing of the Borish experience, she was told by her boss, Frank Newberry, vice president in charge of new products and a cycle enthusiast, to look into using cycles to add time period analysis to econometric analysis.

By the time Shirk left Westinghouse to work for Ford Motor Company as an analyst in marketing, she had learned enough to feel she was bringing the tool of cycle analysis to her new tasks, but she was in for the same kind of treatment that Dewey had experienced. "In the automobile industry, cycles was a naughty word," she said. This, was in the days before Lee Iacocca, a proponent of cycles, surfaced as a power in Detroit. Moreover, Shirk sensed the same kind of conservatism, which would be called discrimination, with respect to the employment and promotion of women. It was not long before she packed her bags, went back to Pittsburgh, and signed on with Dewey for the duration of her career.

Shirk attested to the fascination of cycles. She told me, "One of the considerations I had in looking for a new job when I left Ford was that I never wanted to be bored. Any job has a lot of dog work, of course, but overall the work at the Foundation was never, ever boring." In addition to seeking out and testing cycles through statistical analysis, Shirk became the voice of cycles as editor of the Foundation's magazine. Hers could be a delightfully blunt voice. When, for instance, I asked why there was so much concentration on economics in the Foundation's work, she said, "People are always concerned about money, aren't they? As a matter of fact, writing was invented to take care of numerical transactions, wasn't it?"

However close to the heart, concern about money is itself cyclical, according to Shirk. "Public and professional interest in cycles seems to come and go with the times. When things are prosperous, people are not concerned about a downturn; they think things will go up forever. But when there is a downturn, people are interested in the possibility that it might be rhythmic in nature," she said.

Quite apart from the interest that money-related topics generate, a concentration on economic information in cycle literature is the natural result of an available wealth of data. The recording of economic data extends far back into the history of almost every country, more so than data in any other discipline. In fact, historically, America has paid more attention to business than to that proverbial conversation starter, the weather. Although useful price figures date from 1720, regular meteorological records did not start for another century.

Some cycles in business are so natural and obvious that people make use of them instinctively, such as the recurring seasonal demand for things such as fuel, clothing, toys, and recreational equipment. Although there are some complicating marketing factors, commodities tend to have a structure that follows nature's cycles. Shirk cited soybeans, which have an annual cycle that is 70 percent accurate. In view of the fact that the odds of pure chance are 50-50, an investor who uses a 70-30 predictor as a guide over a long period seems bound to win. There are even more reliable cycles, some of which lurk in the tangle of data produced by the frantic daily trading on Wall Street. These are neither natural nor obvious, and they are usually arrived at by mathematically-minded observers armed with computers. But Anthony F.

Herbst, a professor of finance at the University of Texas who designed an early software program for the Foundation, rated the accuracy of computer-assisted cycle analysis thus: "On a scale of one to ten with ten being perfect accuracy and one being worthless, I'd say probably seven to nine, in that range. That's very good."

With odds such as this, why aren't there more winners on Wall Street? Why are there so many bankruptcies? Why aren't people breaking down the doors of the Foundation and the offices of commercial cycle analysts? In terms of the numbers of people actively employing cycle theory as compared to the millions upon millions of people involved in business, the cycle might as well still be the Rothschild's secret. (Investors close to the Foundation who heeded its forecast of stock market action in 1987 did very well with their personal funds, as they did again in the most recent recession twenty years later.) There are a number of factors involved in the neglect of cycles, many of which will surface as important themes in the unfolding story of this phenomenon.

The first of these factors is that cycles study has not yet found a firm place in the curriculum of economics—or any other discipline. "In higher education, in economic and statistical analysis, the emphasis is on systems analysis, on econometric analysis rather than on time series themselves," said Shirk. "In courses in economics you study cause and effect. For instance, take copper prices. The thinking goes: Deliveries of copper are going down so expect the price to be cut." Shirk acknowledged an increasing interest in the methodology of time series analysis in academic circles, but people such as Professor Herbst who introduced cycles into college course were still pioneers.

A. Bruce Johnson has taught a course in time series analysis at the University of West Florida for fifteen years. He turned to cycles as a way of dealing with a puzzling paradox. "When I first got interested in the stock market, I found the news misleading," he recalled. "If a piece of good economic news comes out, instead of the market responding positively it responds in a negative way. There must be something more to this than just economic news and economic forecasts—the fundamentals, that is. That something else is mass psychology which may be expressed as periods of mass optimism and other periods of mass pessimism regardless of the economic outlook, and they appear to go in cycles. Now I say forget the news and try cycles."

Paul A. Volcker, a former chairman of the Federal Reserve and one of President Obama's chief economic advisers, seemed to share Johnson's feeling that cycles might reflect the human element in the economic data. When Volcker delivered the 1978 Moskowitz Lecture, "The Rediscovery of the Business Cycle," his remarks were prompted by the shock of a 1970s recession that seemed to come out of nowhere, stemming an economic tide that had been rising steadily since World War II. "The evidence seems to be pretty clear that there is some tendency toward swings in the tempo and mood of business activity over relatively long periods of time—say periods of ten to twenty years," he told his audience:

> Those swings may be influenced by a variety of more or less objective events, such as changes in population, wars and their aftermath, waves of technological innovation, and so on. But those

swings also appear to be influenced by less tangible, even psychological phenomena. Specifically, a long period of prosperity breeds confidence, and confidence breeds new standards of what is prudent.

For a while, the process is self-reinforcing, sustaining investment and risk taking. But it may also contain some of the seeds of its own demise: Eventually natural limits to some of the trends supporting the advance are reached, and the advance cannot be sustained so easily. We find ourselves with more houses and shopping centers and oil tankers and steel capacity than we can readily absorb. Financial positions are extended, and the economy has become more vulnerable to adverse and unexpected developments.

As a result we find that a business setback is not coped with so easily by policy changes that served so well in a more buoyant underlying environment. So the mood turns conservative and uncertain: We rediscover the business cycle. Viewed in this light, we need look no further than human nature to find some explanation for recurrent swings in business activity and in a market economy.

Volcker put a twist on Gertrude Shirk's blunt statement about turning to cycles in times of trouble. He also recognized another facet of human nature that would like to rule out cycles: People, especially those with political motivations, want to believe good news will go on forever. The Republican administration's chant after 1929 that "prosperity is just around the corner" is still a bitter memory for many, but Volker quoted more recent pronouncements in the same key. Arthur Oken, who was named Chairman of the Council of Economic Advisers in 1968, was quoted by Volcker as saying, "When recessions were a regular feature of the economic environment, they were often viewed as inevitable. . . . Recessions are now generally considered fundamentally preventable, like airplane crashes and unlike hurricanes." Or listen to an earlier Council Chairman, Walter Heller, who said in 1969 that there was "a constantly deepening conviction in the business and financial community that alert and active fiscal-monetary policy will keep the economy operating at a higher proportion of its potential in the future than in the past; that beyond short and temporary slowdowns, or perhaps even a recession, that's not ruled out in this vast and dynamic economy of ours—lies the prospect of sustained growth in that narrow band around full employment." Volcker noted, too, that in the surging 1960s the Department of Commerce changed the title of its monthly statistical publication from *Business Cycle Developments* to *Business Conditions Digest*. In those optimistic times, cycles were considered dead. Who needed them?

In quoting those statements, Volcker was caught up in a cycle himself, and he was more prescient than he may have known. Another rising economic tide after the low ebb of the early 1980s (which was caused by Volcker's own policy at the Federal Reserve of wringing out inflation) provoked another round of official optimism. In March of 1989, columnist George F. Will wrote of some interesting exchanges during public discussion of shaky bank loans such as the $21 billion that some eleven banks had put out to finance leveraged buyouts. Kenneth J. H. Pinkers of Moody's told Congress that "there *is* a business cycle," and expressed concern about such loans "*when* the business cycle returns." On the other hand, Michael Boskin, another chairman of the Council of Economic Advisers, was quoted as saying that no recession is necessary, that it is a misreading of economic history to suggest that either the frequency or amplitude of recessions is predictable, that he knew of "no economic law mandating that economic expansion died of old age." Columnist Will waffled on the issue. Even as he admitted that Boskin's statements could be true, he pointed out that there had been eight recessions in the past forty years, an average of one every five years.

The debate on the value of cycles would seem to be as eternal and predictable as adherents claim the cycles themselves are. At least one reason for this is clear: Just about anyone engaged in economic activity is reluctant to give up on the econometric models based on cause and effect that dominate the discipline, which is sometimes called a science. For the scholar, they provide a way of organizing and manipulating data to arrive at a rational thesis. For businesspeople, they offer theoretical support to a desire to feel in control of both personal and corporate destiny. For economic advisers, they document the pleasing reassurance that leaders can have the power to improve the economy by following certain policies. The thought that an uncontrollable cycle can wipe out an intellectual construction cemented with research and logic like a tide can crumble a stone seawall is threatening. Yet it happens all the time. Consider another example from Volcker regarding the recession of the 1970s: "Econometric models of consumer behavior no longer seem to fit the facts of the emerging situation. For example, the consumption function developed by Albert Ando and Franco Modigliani for the FRB-MIT-Penn model overpredicted consumption by $6 billion in mid-1973, and by about $13 billion by the end of that year—a sizable error." Still, it runs contrary to human nature to expect that people who have invested a great deal of money or who have painstakingly acquired reputations as experts in the system will surrender their conviction that they should be able to manage either to their taste and advantage.

It is fascinating to write this history of fumbling financial expertise on a March day in 2009 when I can look up from my keyboard and see flickering images of President Obama's economic advisers talking away in an effort to do something about the human element that Volcker acknowledged so long ago as the most important factor in a recession. Interestingly, almost every other word in a talk by Lawrence Summers is related to banishing fear in the population is "cycles." But I have yet to see official credit being given to cycles students for their prescience in forecasting this crisis. Except for its size, the whole scenario surrounding this most recent recession is so like that of those preceding as to confirm its cyclical nature.

The reason that cycle enthusiasts get no credit is that, more often than not, they are looked upon as bearers of bad news, and the fate of such messengers is well known. The most dramatic instance of this in cycle history took place not in capitalistic America but in Communist Russia. During the 1920s, economist Nikolai Kondratieff set out to prove the instability of capitalism through a detailed study of prices, wages, interest rates, foreign trade, bank deposits, and other economic data, as well as factors related to social and cultural life in capitalistic countries throughout the nineteenth century. Kondratieff concluded that capitalism was subject to periodic recessions, but he claimed that it also enjoyed periodic highs. What he saw in the data was a wave of between fifty and fifty-six years duration undulating up and down—a visualization known in cycle circles as the Kondratieff Wave, the K-wave, or the long wave. Stalin, who wanted a prediction that capitalism was doomed, found the Kondratieff message so distasteful that he banished the messenger to Siberia and finally to the firing squad. It is one of the more delicious ironies of history that Stalin's economics were submerged by perestroika while Kondratieff's wave goes on cresting.

In an odd way, Dewey's discovery of cycles two decades later mirrored Kondratieff's. He, too, was working for the government in the midst of the Great Depression to find out why capitalism had suffered such a crippling blow. Before he could reach any conclusions, he was swept out of his office in the Commerce Department by the broom of the New Deal. The assignment did, however, give Dewey an opportunity to talk to economists all over the country. As he later told Gertrude Shirk, he was disappointed to learn of wide disagreement in the field and that no economist could elucidate the causes of the depression clearly enough to stop it from happening again in the future. Dewey's quest gained clarity when he encountered Chapin Hoskins, who was then in the business of cycle analysis. Hoskins told Dewey, "I can't tell you *why* depressions happen, but I can tell you *when* they will." Dewey went to work with Hoskins on what was the beginning of a lifelong search for both the why and when of cycles.

If optimists and economic activists resist using cycles in their monetary affairs, so do the intellectually lazy. Stone's prescription for making millions with the use of cycles rather significantly included the order to "daily engage in creative, positive thinking time." As with any effort to create a model or abstraction of a living organism, the cycle analyst has to find a way through a tangle of ambiguities, contradictions, surprises, and disappointments. Bafflement begins with acknowledging that there is no such thing as a single cycle at work in any given situation.

Even before the computer was available to ferret out the multiplicity of cycles in a mound of data, Harvard's Joseph Schumpter noted in his seminal and monumental work *Business Cycles* that "there is no reason why the cyclical process of evolution should give rise to just one movement. On the contrary, there are many reasons to expect that it will set into motion an indefinite number of wavelike fluctuations which will roll on simultaneously and interfere with one another in the process. Nor does the impression we derive from any graph of economic time series lend support to a single-cycle hypothesis. It is much more natural to assume the presence of many fluctuations of different span and intensity, which seem to be superimposed on each other." Schumpter's assumptions have become gospel today in light of what tools for statistical analysis are revealing, as well as from the reflection of broader theoretical concepts on the nature of cycles.

Among the cycles that have to be taken under consideration in business are the K-wave and a newer long wave theory postulated by R. N. Elliot based on the observation that there is a natural ebb and flow of human economic activity. There are a variety of shorter cycles that might be relevant to the product or market in question. These days a cycle analyst tends to ponder the increasing evidence that economic cycles may be linked to natural cycles such as solar activity. Because the graphs of solar-planetary activity show periodicities similar to those in the markets, a theory has developed that cycles in energy from the Sun are a factor in the "psychological phenomena" that Volcker saw in the markets. The key to correct analysis, according to Richard Mogey, is to "know where you are within a basket of cycles."

The basket is a full one. Using hourly, daily, and weekly data, Mogey proved that at least 230 cycles in the stock market are statistically valid. But statistical validity only tells the analyst that the cycle is probably not random. "Statistical validity isn't as significant as importance," Mogey explained. "I'm interested in the fewer number of cycles that account for the greatest movement in the market. It's a little like the situation where 20 percent of your business brings 80 percent of the profits. There are what I call economic cycles and cycles unique to the market you are dealing with. In seasonal markets, for instance, take soybeans. In the soybean market you will not find a lot of short little cycles. Six months after the beans are in the ground, they know what the crop will be and therefore the market becomes immune to short term variation."

Mogey claims that deciding which cycles are in control of a given market at a given time is a fairly straightforward process that involves a number of established steps and techniques. One of the most important of these is to determine a cycle's history. "It's just like a doctor taking a patient's history," he said. "If you have blood pressure of 90 over 130 the doctor might think it's high. But if, in fact, your blood pressure had been 100 over 150 he might take a different view of it. So in the same way you have to know about the cycle. Every cycle produces a change above and below the trend of an approximate percentage. Looking at the whole data, you must know what the mean change was for that cycle, and you also have to know what the deviations have been and whether or not that cycle is ever a part of another cycle."

Mogey cited the hypothetical case of a thirty-week cycle and a ten-week cycle. If you're looking at a thirty-week cycle and find another cycle with similar phasing three times, or every ten weeks, within it, the ten-week cycle has to be a part of the thirty-week one. Ten is a harmonic of thirty, i.e., 3 x 10 = 30, so these cycles can be seen as part of the same system whereas nine- or eleven- or twelve-week cycles could not. When examined, the history of the ten-week cycle might show a mean percentage change in amplitude (or height) of seven with deviations as high as nine above and ten below. If this cycle goes over 9 percent or down to 11 percent, chances are that another cycle is at work. If the cycle fails to turn as it has in the past, chances are that another cycle is dominant. In this case, according to Mogey, it is a 90-percent certainty that another cycle has taken over.

Aside from the number of cycles involved, the analyst has to determine from history what might be called the cycle's probable shape. Although the sine wave is often used as a model for a cycle, it is inadequate. The sine wave is supposed to move 50 percent above and 50 percent below a given line over a period of time. A two-year cycle that behaved like a sine wave would be expected to go up a year and down a year whereas in the market, as Mogey explained, "a real two-year pattern probably moves up a year and a half and probably goes sideways and down for less time." Out of his long and close study of cyclical history, Mogey recommended paying close attention to the down- side of cycles. His reading of the market movement in 1987 is illustrative:

It was a three-and-a-half-year cycle that topped in July of 1987, and that assumes a year and a half or year and three quarter up and the same time down. But when the cycle high came so close to the exact high it told me that chances were that the low would come very early in the cycle. It's a tendency I've observed. I knew that the market wasn't going to go down for a year and three quarters. This just doesn't happen, even in the worst times. The market barely did it back in the 1930s. So the chances were that there would be rallies in between. By the same token, when the market continues to go higher after the ideal topping time, the chances are that the low will be on time, but that you learn from taking careful history.

In the actual event, Gertrude Shirk's very cautious reading of the puzzling approximately forty-one-month cycle made it possible for alert Foundation members to take advantage of the 1987 crash. This is the cycle that, in Dewey's words, could "keep scientists humble." Acknowledging that the cycle had flip-flopped after World War II, Shirk nevertheless said, in her landmark *Cycles* article of March 1987, that "in spite of this latter day anomaly, subsequent analysis using a weighted moving average to filter the data more precisely, confirmed the 40.68-month period as a statistically significant cycle. The next benchmark on the cycle is at July 1987. This point in time is the critical month around which actual prices will reveal whether or not the cycle is again effective. July 1987 is not a forecast—it is the checkpoint against which we can measure the behavior of the forty-point-sixty-eight-month cycle." Experienced cycle watchers were not fooled by her caution and knew better than to stay in the market much beyond that "critical month."

Complicated as it may sound, cycle analysis for business purposes can be learned by doing. Obviously, it would help to have a good grasp of—or at least a keen interest in—mathematics as well as some computer literacy. Software available from the Foundation should facilitate do-it-yourself analysis, but nobody claims it will be easy. It certainly is not a matter of rote learning or mechanical methods. A great deal of judgment and/or intuition is involved. When A. Bruce Johnson first introduced planetary cycles into his mix of statistical cycles and other economic factors, he got a nearly perfect forecast of the movement on the New York Stock Exchange for 1988, but it went awry in 1989. He took the setback philosophically. There are thirty-six planetary cycles, according to Johnson, who was still experimenting with selecting the five or six most influential ones to use in a composite for forecasting. "Cycles is still an art and still needs lots of work, but it is the only way to go," he insisted. In the last twenty years, research has turned Johnson's artful beginning into more of a science than an art, and the Foundation has made available to researchers a planetary data module.

Fortunately, a technical mastery of cycle analysis is not necessary for anyone who wants to use it in business or investment. The results of a variety of analyses can be obtained from the Foundation or from private practitioners. What is needed is an attitude about cycles. Knowing that cycles are out there when you are dealing with problems in economics is analogous to knowing that doctors are available for consultation when you have health problems. An interesting aspect of this analogy is that medicine is often referred to as an art rather than a science, even by its wiser practitioners. Nevertheless, most people go to doctors, and cycle believers are incredulous

when they encounter the unfortunately widespread ignorance or indiffer-
ence on the part of people who could benefit directly from the faith cycle
believers espouse.

Examples abound, but a fairly typical one was recited to me by former
Foundation managing director Bosley. Because of the damage droughts had
been doing, the Foundation had started to collect data on drought cycles in
the Midwest. When I talked to Bosley, the Foundation had some 48,000
weather observations dating from 1865. One of the sources for this data was
a utility company that had it on a computer disk. Bosley was so delighted
with the "find" that he approached another utility in the hope of obtaining
similar data. He was told by the company's marketing department that "by
law we have to keep six years of data but we don't fuss with that stuff." The
story was totally believable to me as I had tried to get records from my own
water company dating back only five years and discovered that they had
vanished into thin air. I also found Bosley's reasoning flawless. "On which of
these two companies would you bet?" he asked. "The first company has to
be given an A for coming up with that data and working with it to anticipate
the demands that could be put upon them."

When it comes to appropriating the Rothschild's secret for personal use,
a conversation I had with Richard Mogey is worth repeating:

> Q—Can an ordinary citizen use cycle analysis?
> A—The average person couldn't analyze the cycles. It takes
> a good deal of training in statistics and computers to do it. But
> people with computers can get a program from the Foundation
> and try to produce an analysis themselves. It's like anything else—

some people are better at it than others. I've never done anything that there wasn't somebody better than I.

Q—What's *your* batting average on analysis?

A—Somewhere between 80 and 90 percent. I think that's about what you can expect out of cycles. But back to your original question, the average citizen can use what comes out of cycle analysis. For instance, if he or she had known that sometime in July or August of 1987 there would be a major drop in the market that would have been very useful information. That's why we have a membership magazine.

Cycles are concerned with timing, and most brokerage houses are not. The last thing they want to see is everybody out of the stock market. It's not in their self-interest to tell people we are going to have bad times for the next two years, and you shouldn't be investing in stocks. So they've taken another tack—and it's a reasonable tack. They say they're going to find the best quality stock for you in terms of company performance, and some of them do a very good job at this. Stock picking and timing are two different things. Most of the major brokerage houses are focused on stock picking.

An investor has to be very clear about his objectives. The average investor is much better off buying and holding except in major moves of the market. So there's a certain degree of timing. To have been in good stocks in 1982 and gotten out early in 1987 would have been perfect.

As Mogey's comments indicate, cycle theory is not a guide to quick killings in business or the markets, nor is it advice on how to outsmart everybody else. That it was once a secret of the repeatedly successful Rothschilds seems symbolic. The real secret of cycles as a business tool was spelled out by Dan Ascani, editor of the *Elliot Wave Commodity Forecast,* in an article for *Cycles*:

> The natural laws of the universe remind us once again that, for every action, there is a reaction. For every upwave, there is a downwave. For every expansion, there is a contraction. For every bull market, there is a bear market. Survival comes to those who understand, accept, and prepare for these natural swings.

No resource has a better record of success in preparing for these up- and downswings than the Foundation for the Study of Cycles. In what might be called a cyclic repeat of its performance in 1987, the Foundation issued warnings many months ahead of what would take place in the stock market in 2008. The first came through an article in Barron's Online by Michael Kane on April 16, 2008, in which he quoted the Foundation as saying that the market was "due to bottom in November." A second was passed along in a mass e-mail from the Foundation that predicted a "Dow election day roller coaster and an inaugural day crash."

The Foundation was not alone in its reading of cycles. Commodity trader Jake Bernstein said, "In the late 1960s I discovered the power and potential of cycles and seasonals. I saw a copy of *Cycles* magazine. It changed my life forever and very much for the better. It's been an amazing and productive forty-year journey for me."

Much of the productive part has come from using cycles when predicting the future of the markets. In this case, as Bernstein informed me, "When prices exploded and the cycles were topping, a host of timing indicators told me that a large collapse was coming, and I advised my clients of such giving them specific indicators that led me to that conclusion. Prior to September 2008 and then again on September 27, 2008, I went on record with Webinars showing my logic and giving my forecasts."

Following the money through cycles leads to the very sober and thought-provoking conclusion that no amount of economic planning will restore the golden days of SUVs in every driveway and McMansions on every block. Back in the '90s, Richard Mogey, then executive director of the Foundation, sorted through his basket of cycles and came up with a reliable twenty-year cycle in real estate that enabled him to write an article in *Cycles* predicting a peak in values in 2006 and a decline until a bottoming out in 2016.

In an article in the *New York Times* about physicists who left academia to try their scientific skills in the market, Dennis Overbye wrote: "As Dr. [Emmanuel] Derman put it in his book *My Life as a Quant: Reflection on Physics and Finance*, 'In physics there may one day be a Theory of Everything; in finance and the social sciences, you're lucky if there is a usable theory of anything.'" I can only hope that one day Derman will read this book.

Chapter Four

Nature on the Move

During the frigid January of 2009, there was a joke making the rounds in Connecticut: "Where is global warming when you need it?" The unusual nature of the cold that month sticks in my mind more because of a feature story I read in the paper than any statistics on temperature. As a sailing enthusiast, I was interested to learn that ice boats were racing on the Hudson River for the first time in years. The fact that one of the boats was more than 100 years old and still in condition to compete would indicate how infrequently weather conditions were favorable for its use.

An astute student of cycles would not be bewildered by the paradox of a rare cold patch during what is thought to be a time of alarming warming. There are cycles within cycles in a universe always on the move, and the unexpected is most likely to be encountered in one of the most active aspects of this movement—weather. Another Connecticut resident, Mark Twain, said of New England weather that it was "always doing something." But even in more equable climates, the weather is busy. In the Virgin Islands there is almost perpetual sunshine and very little temperature change throughout the year, but I have seen four or five quick showers in an hour, and there are occasional devastating hurricanes. Like the rest of cycle-driven nature, the weather is continually surprising—and beyond our control.

Weather—an uncontrollable force—has more immediate effect on human activity than any other natural movement. It ranges from governing what we wear each day to what, and whether, we eat. Out of necessity human beings have always been acutely aware of weather, and the annals of history are steeped in references to weather conditions. During the millennia when travel and communication were limited to the horizon for the bulk of humanity, people developed an instinctive wisdom about the weather around them and passed it on in sayings such as "red sky at night sailor's delight; red sky in the morning sailors take warning." But it was not until 1743 that Benjamin Franklin became the first person to note that weather moves: On a September day he reported that a storm he experienced in Philadelphia moved up to Boston. It took more than another century before the U.S. Signal Corps set up the first national weather service in 1870. From then until 1933, when Henry Wallace became Secretary of Agriculture, no government forecast was made more than twenty-four hours in advance. With several generations of farmers in his family, Wallace pressed for at least a forty-eight-hour forecast.

There are so many variables—cycles within cycles—involved in weather's movement that it took the birth of the computer to turn the study and prediction of weather into a major enterprise involving uncalculated expense and time. In addition to private businesses, there is an alphabet soup of U.S. government agencies at work on weather. To wit: NOAA, National Oceanic and Atmospheric Administration; OAR, Office of Oceanic and Atmospheric Research; NESDIS, National Environmental Satellite and Data Information Service; NWS, National Weather Service; NOS, National Ocean Service; NMFS, National Marine Fisheries; WG1, Working Group I, which assesses the physical scientific aspects of the climate system and climate change; and WG2, Working Group II, which assesses the vulnerability of socioeconomic and natural systems to climate change, negative and positive consequences of climate change, and options for adapting to it. Because weather occurs worldwide, so are the agencies dealing with it: IPCC, Intergovernmental Panel on Climate Change, shared the Nobel Peace Prize in 2007 with the apostle of global warming, former U.S. Vice President, Albert A. Gore, Jr.

Thanks to the computer, technology has given the people who put their heads together to catch weather on the fly some amazing tools. In Princeton, New Jersey, there is an organization called the Geophysical Fluid Dynamics Laboratory under the aegis of NOAA where two $25 million supercomputers, tended by a large team of scientists, run around the clock in an attempt to cope with billions of numbers in simulations of global weather and climate. A measure of the complexity facing these researchers is that the printout of a single model can be as large as a metropolitan telephone book, contain as many as 30,000 lines of computer code and take ten years to write. In an early report on G.F.D.L.'s operation, a writer for *Princeton Alumni Weekly*, J. I. Merritt explained the process:

A model divides the atmosphere into a vast three-dimensional grid comprising tens of thousands of rectangular boxes. Each box contains a set of equations representing the laws of motion and thermal dynamics governing fluid systems, and each set of equations includes such meteorological variables as wind speed and direction, temperature, barometric pressure, humidity, and incoming solar radiation. A box reflects the conditions of its particular space, taking into account the effects of latitude, vegetation, topography, and cloud cover. Every box is linked mathematically to its neighbors, so that changes in one affect the solutions of equations in others. A model represents the atmosphere at a point in time. Once the initial conditions are set, the computer can begin solving the model's equations. Like a time-lapse film, a model runs many times faster than reality, in a matter of minutes or hours projecting scenarios for conditions a week, a season, or even decades into the future.

Because even the best of models are not living weather, surprises keep coming. One model that the G.F.D.L. scientists created to predict the impact of greenhouse warming by the year 2050 called for drier summers in the southeastern Great Lakes and plain states while another concluded that they would be wetter. No wonder one scientist called weather "a horrendous complicated mess." But such puzzles notwithstanding, computer-assisted analysis of the history of weather has established some reliable laws governing weather that could be the basis for an improvement in forecasting. To the surprise of nobody in cycleland, one of these laws is the tendency of weather-making factors to recur in cycles.

Had he lived to learn of it, Edward R. Dewey would have welcomed this confirmation of an assumption he arrived at many years earlier. While carrying out its self-appointed mission of extracting statistically viable cycles from any available data bank, Foundation researchers managed to identify a number of recurring patterns that had an obvious bearing on weather. Mainly because the records were available, the Foundation studied barometric pressure in New York from 1873 through 1967. Dewey always took the position that the organization's mission was to identify cycles wherever they appeared, regardless of their apparent significance or lack thereof. In this case, the potential usefulness of a barometric cycle was almost self-evident in that barometric pressure is an acknowledged predictor of weather. There are, in Dewey's calculation, about 5 quadrillion tons of atmosphere bearing down on Earth with an air pressure at sea level of 14.7 pounds per square inch, or 1 ton per square foot. The barometer records this pressure as inches of mercury, and 29.91 such inches equal 14.7 pounds of air pressure per square inch. When the mercury rises, the weather turns fair; when it falls, it turns foul. From the barometer readings in New York, the Foundation plotted a graph that formed a 7.6-year cycle in barometric pressure at five widely separated weather stations around the world.

Another weather cycle that Dewey reported had to do with what he called "the rhythm of the rain." Working with figures from 1820 to 1960 of recorded rainfall in Philadelphia, the Foundation discovered a 4.33-year cycle in precipitation. Follow-up analysis of data for New York and Baltimore produced exactly the same figure. Less authoritative but very intriguing to Dewey was a finding by E. G. Bowen, Chief of the Radiophysics Division of the Commonwealth Scientific and Industrial Organization in Australia, that it rained so regularly on January 13 in Brisbane as to be more probable than chance—a finding corroborated by a U.S. Weather Bureau study showing a recurring high and low rainfall pattern on the same calendar days. Dewey also expressed considerable confidence in the 35-year Bruckner cycle of wet oceanic and dry continental European weather, Ellsworth Huntington's 9.66-year cycle of atmospheric ozone as measured in London and Paris between 1877 and 1910, and Raymond H. Wheeler's 100-year climatic cycle coinciding with tree rings and the rise and fall of civilizations.

Professor Rhodes Fairbridge, a Columbia University geologist and consultant to NASA's Goddard Institute for Space Studies, and Theodore Landscheidt, director of the Schroeter Institute for Research in Cycles of Solar Activity, came up with evidence that the movements of the Moon and Sun that control Earth's tides also have a correlation with—if not a controlling effect upon—Earth's climate. To the extent that these observations can be enlarged upon and proved in practice, both short-term and long-term forecasting can become more accurate. Some heavenly cycles last a century or more, and all of them are more predictable than those in the atmosphere and oceans. They are not, however, entirely regular because there is an elusive dynamics in celestial activity as well as in terrestrial fluids. The Sun's planets do what may be described as a form of dance around each other in which their movements are determined by interaction as with partners on a ballroom floor.

Landscheidt used one cosmic dance step in particular to illustrate the hypothesis that solar events do correlate with weather: It is an alignment of Jupiter, the center of mass, and the Sun's center that he calls JU-CM-CS. This alignment is cyclical because it recurs in rhythms that vary from two to sixteen years. Checked against a graph of yearly rainfall in Germany between

1851 to 1983, it developed that JU-CM-CS epochs coincided with peaks in precipitation.

Fairbridge published a paper in *Quaternary Science Reviews*, cowritten with Robert Guinn Currie of the State University of New York at Stony Brook, that, used climatic references in China's unique written history to come up with a more than coincidental connection between heavenly happenings and recurring floods and droughts in China. Their conclusion: "Analysis of a drought-flood index for Peking (Beijing) in northeastern China since A.D. 1470 supports evidence for both periodic lunar nodal 18.6-year and solar cyclic 11-year induced drought-flood in the region." The Moon's nodal cycle begins and ends at the points where its orbit intersects the elliptic, the plane of the Earth's orbit; the Sun's 11-year cycle is the periodic waxing and waning of sunspots.

The importance to Fairbridge and his colleagues of their investigations is that "they may serve perhaps to illustrate what is now beginning to emerge as a great new paradigm of twentieth century science: the exogenic theory of climate." *Exogenic* simply means originating from the outside. In this case, it is used to indicate that forces from outside of Earth's atmosphere cause changes in climate and associated weather.

With this in mind, it would seem essential to take celestial cycles into consideration in the debate about the "greenhouse effect."

The name is most appropriate according to Professor Fairbridge who said, "If you possess a greenhouse in the back of your home, you know how it warms up in sunshine. If you raise the carbon dioxide, or CO_2 in the atmosphere, the CO_2 tends to raise the water vapor, and the two together raise the heat-retaining capacity of atmosphere like the glass over the greenhouse." CO_2 is released into the atmosphere by a number of natural processes, but since the Industrial Revolution and the onrush of modern civilization, unnatural, man-made processes such as the burning of fossil fuels and the release of chemicals found in spray cans is upsetting the natural atmospheric balance.

Since scientists have detected an abnormally rapid rate of increase in atmospheric CO_2 in the last sixty years, an alarming scenario has been concocted. Greenhouse warming might cause such things as flooding from oceans swelled by melting polar ice caps and/or encroaching desert in the food belts of the world.

Although nobody denies the possibility that this scenario could play itself out, the vagaries of weather and climate that make it so fascinating and frustrating at the same time cause the scientists most directly concerned with the atmosphere to be more cautious than politicians or alarmed environmentalists. If you were to make a phrase encompassing all the information I have absorbed about the greenhouse effect from reading and talking to experts, it would be this: Just about anything can happen. Remember the different results that the G.F.D.L. laboratory got from their two models for 2050? There are many, many factors besides carbon dioxide content that influence the heat retaining capacity of the atmosphere. One is clouds. Those fluffy white cumulous clouds of a summer day reflect back heat into space while high-altitude cirrus clouds let sunlight through and trap heat.

"How we treat cloud cover in our models can affect by a factor of two the impact of a doubling in atmospheric carbon dioxide," G.F.D.L. scientist Syukuro Manabe told *Princeton Alumni Weekly*. "There are all kinds of cloud types, and to model them accurately we need to know how their optical qualities would change with increasing levels of carbon dioxide. Our knowledge in this area is deficient, and until we know more and can incorporate this knowledge into the models, we have to be humble in our predictions."

But an even more important—and also quite variable—factor is the Sun itself, because the Sun is the source of any and all heat. Both Fairbridge and Landscheidt predicted the inception of a new, prolonged minimum of solar activity sometime between 1990 and 2013. Whether the prediction may be coming true as of this writing is not certain, but time has not yet run out. Previous periods have lasted as long as fifty years or more. Professor Fairbridge spelled out for me what this could mean:

> In a study made with Shirley (James H. Shirley, a solar physicist), we came to the conclusion that the Sun's orbit around the barycenter of the solar system has a direction of symmetry. When it comes back to the starting point something like once every 178-odd years we find that there is a minimum of solar activity. In the past when that happened we saw "little ice age" conditions. In the last little ice age, mean winter temperatures in New England dropped about four degrees Celsius, or eight degrees Fahrenheit. It was highly noticeable. There were small fluctuations of this sort from 1805 to 1825 approximately, and New York Harbor and the East River froze repeatedly for long periods of time. It was reported that an ox was roasted in the middle of the East River. In Britain during one ice age, they held fairs on the frozen Thames River, and there's a picture of Henry VIII and his entourage riding on horseback from Hampton Court to Westminster down the middle of the Thames.

The arrival of this next ice age should, in theory, counteract the greenhouse warming. But because of the many variables, Professor Fairbridge would not hazard a guess as to what will actually happen. He emphasized the role oceans play in the atmosphere. Atmospheric CO_2 is in equilibrium with CO_2 in the oceans, which is always changing. Take Fairbridge's ice age scenario as he outlined it to me:

> As you lower temperatures, particularly in high latitudes, it would increase wind velocity which would increase the strength of the jet stream. This would raise the organic activity—the metabolic rate of organisms living on the surface of the warm waters of the ocean. In this process, these organisms would consume more CO_2 which would tend to cool the Earth further. But if the Earth gets warmer due to the greenhouse effect, less CO_2 will be consumed by organisms in a sluggish ocean and more will be liberated into the atmosphere, making it warmer still. I have no idea which direction it will go.

This uncertainty should not suggest that human beings stop the gathering momentum worldwide to curb man-made pollution, particularly from the burning of fossil fuels such as oil and coal. As in other aspects of this cycle story, I am prompted to make a comparison with medicine, which is so often called an art rather than a science. Art can encompass an intuitive wisdom that is lacking in a science pridefully based on so-called absolute proof. I am specifically reminded of a conversation I had with the former Surgeon General of the United States, Dr. C. Everett Koop, when I was working with him on an antismoking article. I had just given up the habit myself after more than forty-eight years of smoking once every waking hour, and I was still looking for a rationale to go back to that craved comfort. Because my father who smoked and lived to the age of ninety-two, I asked Dr. Koop if a genetic intolerance for smoke wasn't the real cause of cancer rather than the substance itself. Conceding that this *might* be true, Dr. Koop said, "You would be one of the lucky ones, but from what we know today, to go on smoking is like playing Russian roulette with your life." I have not smoked since, and so I am personally inclined to agree with scientists who advise us to play it safe with the atmosphere.

Because of their known exogenous origin, tides are one of Earth's many moving parts that are predictable. As Dr. Jeff Horovitz told me when he was director of the Foundation for the Study of Cycles, "Tides are the greatest example of the kind of thing we study." The greatest student of tides on the Foundation's roster was the late Fergus J. Wood whose outstanding scholarly accomplishment *Tidal Dynamics: Coastal Flooding and Cycles of Gravitational Force* remains a classic in cycle literature. Wood's procedure and persistence in pursuing his investigations were classics of scholarship, as well.

Wood was an astronomer by discipline. After graduating from the University of California at Berkeley with a degree in astronomy in 1938, he did postgraduate work at California, Chicago, and Michigan universities until his studies were interrupted by World War II. Commissioned by the AAF Technical Training Command, he received special training at the Institute of Meteorology, University of Chicago, and served as a flight weather officer throughout the war. His postwar career included stints of teaching at the universities of Maryland and Johns Hopkins; service as Aeronautical and Space Research Scientist and Scientific Assistant to the Director, Office of

Space Flight Programs, NASA; and Research Associate, Office of the Director, National Ocean Survey, National Oceanic and Atmospheric Administration.

In 1962, while Wood was working for the U.S. Coast and Geodetic Service before moving on to NOAA, there was a tidal disaster along the east coast of the United States of historic proportions. In two and a half days between March 6 and 8, flooding at high tide claimed forty lives and destroyed some $500 million worth of property. "I thought there was more than met the eye in that flooding event," Wood told me. "We knew that there was a strong wind present which made possible the actual flooding. But what made possible the actual high tides which in turn made possible the cupping action which in turn made possible the sweeping of waves toward shore?"

Being an astronomer, Wood started looking for answers up in the skies. The relationship between the Moon and tides is the kind of natural knowledge we all absorb as children. Anybody living near tidal waters has an intuitive understanding of them. Tides vary visibly with the phases of the Moon in a rhythm that is nearly as regular as that of day following night. The mechanism involved is the force of gravity. This force holds the heavenly bodies in orbit around each other, and the closer they are the stronger it is. The Moon, our nearest neighbor, exerts more of this force than any other heavenly body. This force is neither even nor regular. Although the tides do rise and fall in a twice daily rhythm, their range varies according to gravitational forces. Twice a month—at new moon and full moon—the Earth, Moon, and Sun are in alignment. Astronomers call this alignment syzygy (pronounced siz-a-gee). In syzygy, the Sun's lesser gravitational pull is added to the Moon's stronger one to create what are known as spring tides. The word "spring" has nothing to do with the season but is descriptive of the tide's action in rising higher and faster. Like the Earth's orbit of the Sun, the Moon's orbit of the Earth is not circular but elliptical. Once each revolution, at a point on its orbit known as perigee (closest to Earth), the Moon's gravitational pull will be stronger than normal. Either syzygy or perigee will raise tides by about 20 percent above normal. But when, infrequently, they come within a day and a half of each other, their combined increase in force creates a perigean spring tide that is 40 percent higher.

Beyond these rather well-known variations, there are many different degrees of perigee that cause further fluctuations. If it is separated by only a matter of hours from syzygy—quite a rare event—the resulting gravitational force draws the Moon into an exceptionally close orbit and raises tides even higher. This would not be a negligible increase. Contemplating the 1962 disaster, Wood had a hunch that something such as this must have happened. If so, the greater amount of water lifted into the path of the strong wind blowing at that time would account for the flooding. Unfortunately for people caught in subsequent floods, it was not until he moved to NOAA in 1973 that Wood was given the time and facilities to follow up on his hunch.

Wood began his study by asking the Naval Observatory in Washington to use its mainframe computers to provide a listing of all instances of perigee-syzygee coincidences back to year 1600. With these dates in hand, Wood buried himself in the Library of Congress to see what might have been recorded in the way of tides, weather, and flooding. It proved to be a thrilling exercise. "It was like popping pieces into a jigsaw puzzle," he recalled. Eventually, Wood came up with one hundred cases of major tidal flooding over a 293-year period that contained all the elements of the 1962 incident and presented a cyclical picture into which 1962 fitted neatly.

In the process of his study, Wood accumulated enough data on what he calls lunisolar cycles to be able to project his tide tables into the year 2164. He was also able to isolate those instances within the cycle of perigee-syzygy alignment when the small time differential resulted in an exceptionally close approach of the Moon to Earth. With due apology to linguists, he borrowed *proximate* from Latin to stand for close, and combined it with Greek *gee* for earth to coin new words to define this situation—i.e., *proxigee-syzygy* and *proxigean spring tide*. What he was learning seemed like new territory to Wood, but he suspected from the history of science that somebody might have been there before him. He did not want to undergo the rigorous labor of turning his findings into a book until he made a computer search of worldwide literature in the field. To his surprise there were no books, and a significant number of the relatively few papers on the subject of tidal flooding dealt with hurricanes, which have their own special characteristics. Wood had come upon a seemingly obvious and logical process of nature that, in his words, "had never been brought to the attention of the public for no known reason."

As a public servant, Wood felt that he could not wait through the long process of writing and publishing a book to share his knowledge. Wood informed the press that according to all calculations, there would be conditions for a repeat of the 1962 flooding in early 1974. Because destructive flooding is produced by a combination of tide and weather, Wood would not issue a "prediction." He was always leery of using that word; he preferred "advisory." The problem is that, while lunisolar cycles controlling tides have long and predictable time intervals, the weather moves in tighter, swifter cycles. The lead on a science story in *Time* for January 7, 1974, reflects both the novelty of Wood's revelations and the caution of his approach:

> If there are severe storms in either the Atlantic or Pacific oceans around January 8, Americans living in coastal areas may well be hit by bad floods. This unusual warning was sounded last week by federal scientists [identified later in the story as Fergus J. Wood]. Why January 8? Because of a relatively rare combination of circumstances, tides will be abnormally high around that time. Although the tides alone will not cause flooding, strong, persistent onshore winds accompanying a coastal storm would pile the water even higher, spilling it into low-lying areas.

In this particular instance, the East Coast was spared because of relatively mild weather. What happened on the West Coast is described by a headline from the *Los Angeles Times* on January 9, 1974: GIANT WAVES POUND SOUTHLAND COAST, UNDERMINE BEACH HOMES. Even with this striking fulfillment of Wood's prophecy, little was made of his warning that the same tidal conditions would return in August. It was not mentioned at all in *Time* or in newspaper articles about the January floods. Fortunately, the tides then were not accompanied by storms, but my personal experience still stands as a dramatic example of what trauma might be spared countless others if Wood's tables ever make their way into mainstream tide and weather reporting. Accurate tide tables are of vital importance to navigators on vessels moving through tidal waters. An error can cause property damage or even lost lives. I learned this the hard way that August when ignorance of a rare but important cyclical event turned out to be far from bliss.

I did not understand why this particular overnight sailing race on Long Island Sound was scheduled to start well after dark. Maybe the organizers' top priority was to enrich their club's treasury with a festive dinner for 100 or so guests preceding the event. More likely it would be more "sporting" than a daylight start. They were right about that!

I was crewing on a thirty-foot sloop from another club. The starting line was established between a buoy and a committee boat—both nothing but dim presences in the pitch black before moonrise—and the area was unfamiliar to us. The skipper assigned tasks as we jockeyed for position behind the line with some twenty other boats ranging from twenty-five to fifty feet in length. We were all trying not to become one of those things that "go bump in the night." Knowing that I had qualified in the U.S. Power Squadron courses for the rating of junior navigator, the skipper asked me to plot our course for after the start and then to time the start.

It seemed like a gift from the gods. During the prestart turmoil and tension, I would be down below studying the charts and out of harm's way. It was breezing up, and at the very last second before the start the deck crew would have to raise the spinnaker. (For those unfamiliar with sailboats, an enormous sail that balloons around the boat's bow and looks beautiful in pictures but is the devil's own job to manage on a boat of any size because of the power it generates.)

We were starting in the mouth of a harbor opening out to the Sound. There was a long spit of sand on our right which we were supposed to round and keep bearing right to head east. These were well-charted waters, and the charts told me the depth of water we could expect under the boat at low tide. My job was to plot a course that would shave as close to the spit as possible without getting into shallow water. A piece of cake. We drew about six feet, and I laid a line that would take us over no less than eight feet at mean low water.

I called the course up to the skipper, set a stopwatch in accordance with the series of guns booming from the committee boat and stood on the companionway steps to call the time to the skipper a few feet above me in the cockpit. With a lot of effort and a little luck, our timing crossing the line was excellent. The crew even cheered. We were on the right side in relation to most of the fleet, but the riding lights and ghostly pillow-shaped spinnakers of several competitors could still be seen between us and the sand spit.

Having stopped the watch, I do not know to this day how long the burst of euphoria over our chances of doing well in the race lasted. It could only have been a few seconds or a few minutes—not longer. Suddenly the boat shuddered to a dead stop. A few surprised crewmen lost their footing. The jolt and the still wind-stretched sails put such a strain on the rigging that a stay popped out of its spreader. We were unmistakably hard aground! Fortunately, there was no grinding of rock beneath the hull; we were in the soft grip of sand. Just before I hit the deck to join in the flurry of activity to get the spinnaker down and rock the boat free, I glanced to starboard and saw that the other boats closer to the sand spit were no longer moving either.

Although we were able to continue, we had lost the advantage of a good start, and we were crippled. It was not a happy voyage as we trailed the rest of the fleet around the course. As navigator and presumably the cause of it all, I was especially miserable, even though our skipper never reproached me. Considering what he stood to lose in face with the racing fraternity, not to mention in money for repairs, I felt that I deserved anything he could think of to call me.

There was some very small consolation in discovering at the end of the race that one of the other boats that had grounded was captained by no less than the commodore of the host club who presumably knew the harbor waters like the back of his hand. But I knew that being a club commodore was not necessarily synonymous with being a good sailor. Thus, I carried with me feelings of failure about that ill-fated voyage for fifteen years until I got involved in writing about cycles.

When I learned from Wood's "advisory" for August 17, 1974, that the tidal range would be an event recurring only twenty times in 300 years, I rushed to the informal journal that I, like most writers, keep. The date coincided with a brief journal notation about the race. So there it was at last! Both the commodore and I had been using smart navigational tactics in blissful ignorance of an abnormal tidal situation that could have been predicted if enough attention was being paid to knowledge that even then was available to people who understand cycles.

My brief grounding in a sailing race is only a small example of what has and still could happen as a result of ignorance about tides. It seems strange that it has taken so long to understand the mechanism of tides as they have written much of the history of all the sea coasts in the world. A tide similar to the one that caught me unawares played a part in the naval war during the American Revolution. The event took place just at the eastern end of the same body of water, Long Island Sound, but on the Connecticut shore. Even as the reverse of a very low tide is a very high one, so in a sense, that eighteenth century tide had a reverse result to mine.

In September 1776, one of the first warships funded by the Continental Congress—the twenty-eight-gun frigate *Trumbull*—was launched from the shipyard of John Cotton in East Middletown, Connecticut. Unwittingly (it's to be hoped), the builders made that classical error of amateurs who construct a boat in the basement and then have to tear a wall down to get it out. The draft of the completed frigate was about eighteen feet; the shallowest water level in the ship channel of the Connecticut River is shown on charts of that time as six to eight feet at mean low tide which means that it would only rise to about twelve feet even on a spring tide. Inevitably, the *Trumbull* grounded on a bar on her way to the Sound. To the chagrin of Congress and no doubt the delight of the British Navy, the *Trumbull* remained stuck on the bar until August 11, 1779, when the same sort of tide that grounded me lifted her. Some indication of how fortunes of war might have been altered is the *Trumbull's* record when she finally did get to sea. She was continually in action—her engagement with the British privateer *Watt* was rated the second worst naval battle of the war—and she was called "the celebrated rebel frigate named *Trumbull*" in a notice of her arrival in New York at the end of her service in the summer of 1781.

After the first edition of Wood's book came out in 1978 with definite proof of his thesis and a table of "advisories" stretching far into the future, the revelations were still largely ignored by weather watchers and coastal

inhabitants alike. Typical of the cost of ignorance were results of tidal flooding along the California coast during January 27 to 31 of 1983 when 2,600
homes and 496 businesses were damaged, 1,964 people were forced to flee,
the Pacific Coast Highway was blocked at more than four places, and piers
collapsed at Seal Beach and Point Arena. Wood was fascinated and disturbed
to note how accounts of current flooding echoed a report he dug up of the
first recorded tidal disaster in American history in 1635.

"This year the 24 or 25 of August was such a mighty storm of wind and
raine [sic] as none living in these parts, either English or Indians, ever saw,"
wrote William Bradford in *History of Plimoth Plantation*. Of the same event
Nathaniel Morton reported in *New England Memorial* that it "blew down
houses and uncovered divers others; divers vessels were lost at sea in it, and
many more in extreme danger. It caused the sea to swell in some places to
southward of Plymoth, as that it arose to twenty feet right up and down, and
made many Indians to climb into trees for their safety. The mark of it will
remain this many years in those parts where it was sorest; the moon suffered
a great eclipse two nights after it."

Wood realized that he had found a classic case of his proxigean spring
tides—a case that turned a wind storm into the kind of flooding that chased
Indians into trees—when he read the mention of an eclipse, the ultimate
syzygy. In view of the way the world has changed in other respects since, it
seems remarkable that flooding still catches its most sophisticated citizens
just as much by surprise. Knowing that weather is as important as tide in
these disasters, a determined Wood joined forces with Irving P. Krick—who,
as the man who advised Eisenhower on the weather for D-Day, was Amer-

ica's most famous forecaster—to see if they could issue a joint "advisory" far enough ahead of a flood to allow people to take evasive or protective action. Armed with charts from the Krick organization showing probable storms with strong onshore winds along both coasts from December 29, 1986, through January 3, 1987, Wood went out on a limb to issue a flooding "advisory" when *USA Today* called him to discuss what they might run in their December 26–28, weekend edition.

Brief excerpts from two newspapers tell the rest of the story. First, the *USA Today* feature: "A triple celestial phenomenon that hasn't occurred in a generation may leave USA coastlines flooded in record tides next week . . . Possible trouble spots: Carolina coasts, Puget Sound, Bay of Main . . ." Next, a story by Dennis Hevesi in the *New York Times*, January 3, 1987:

> A classic northeaster, combined with tides raised unusually high by a rare celestial configuration, sent New Englanders scurrying inland yesterday afternoon after the storm left six people dead and caused at least $14 million in damage along the southeastern coast of the United States . . . In Marshfield, Mass., the tides whipped by winds of up to 60 miles an hour, broke through a sea wall at about noon and trapped hundreds of people. Rescuers used boats and trucks to reach some of the people. People had scrambled onto roofs of their homes, cars or places of business.

Sounds a lot like the Indians in the same state 352 years earlier, doesn't it? And a lot like the people of New Orleans eighteen years later? Apparently discouraged by lack of attention to their successful experiment, Wood and

Krick took their know-how to their graves, and I have been unable to dis-cover any followers in this new millennium.

John Bagby, another student of both gravity and cycles on the Founda-tion roster, was concerned with disasters wrought by earthquakes. Bagby and his wife Loretta spent twenty-five years pondering about, and experi-menting with, such matters as why gravity doesn't work precisely accord-ing to the gospel of Newton. Together, they conducted precise and tedious experiments that led them to conclude, among other things, that planetary cycles are responsible for variations in the effect of gravity, as they are in tides. The gravitational pull the other planets exert on Earth is also a factor in earthquakes in Bagby's view. "What I think about earthquakes," Bagby explained to me, is that:

> the ground builds up a stress, and the stress is going to release at some time. What happens is that the Moon and Sun and planets pull on the Earth and cause it to prematurely trigger the quake. In other words, the quake is going to happen anyway, but these celestial influences, which most scientists think are ridiculously weak, tease the earthquake into going off ahead of time. Because the earthquake is triggered into going off sooner than it would if it was allowed to build up its stress to the breaking point, we have fours, fives, and sixes on the Richter scale instead of having eights, nines, and tens. I look upon the planets and the Moon as a ben-eficial artifact of nature that teases Earth into premature quakes. It's amazing how little energy it takes from these bodies, and no one can really say why theoretically this is so. That's where the problem arises. There is no theory to account for this synergetic effect. It is out of all proportion to the mass of the planet or the Moon or where it is, but when planets line up at certain angles to each other there is this tendency to release energy.

If much is still unknown about this force, the knowledge that makes tides predictable is nevertheless applicable to earthquakes. "This celestial influence is very predictable, and it repeats," Bagby insisted. "Some 33 percent of all earthquakes over 7.3 occur when the Moon is new or full or in the quarter—a cardinal phase. But the other 66 percent of large earthquakes are triggered when the Moon is halfway between, when the Moon's tidal force is most rapidly changing from weak to strong." There is a cyclical nature to earthquakes themselves. For instance, Bagby found that quakes in Armenia fit into a historical eleven-year pattern.

Despite his knowledge and convictions, Bagby was even more reluctant to make "predictions" about specific earthquake occurrences than Wood was about tides. "There's a kind of law against it," he said. "The Geophysical Union and the Geological Society of America both put out bulletins requesting that all of us refrain from making predictions." One reason for this may be the potential havoc that earthquake predictions could create unless they are 100 percent accurate. This he found impossible with the data available to him. Using time series analysis, Bagby could predict when the triggering forces for earthquakes were likely to be present down to the year, month, day, and hour but not where. Knowing that information is the province of geology. "Geologists know where the stresses are but don't cooperate much with people predicting time," he said.

This may change as more data emerges from pursuit of the latest theory about the structure of our planet. Called plate tectonics, it postulates that the seemingly solid earth beneath our feet is made up of huge individual "plates" that are constantly on the move at a creep the slowest snail would envy. Every so often—in time frames that can run to millions of years—plates can collide and erupt into volcanic or earthquake activity. Although it was speculated as early as 1596 that the opposite coasts of the Atlantic Ocean were so shaped as to have once fitted together, it was not until 1912 when Alfred Wegner, a German scientist, came up with the concept of "continental drift" that the studies leading to the birth of plate tectonics in 1956 began. One of the boundaries between plates where friction occurs is the Pacific plate's "ring of fire" where underwater eruptions led to the tsunami in 2004 that, according to Reuters, "left 230,000 people either dead or missing across Asia from Sri Lanka and India to Thailand, the Maldives and Indonesia."

The cyclical nature of that tsunami was long in surfacing. But in 2008, two articles in *Nature* claimed that a similarly devastating tsunami flooded the same region some 600 years earlier. Researchers from Chulalongkorn University in Thailand combed a grassy plain on the island of Phra Thong where the tsunami reached wave heights of 65 feet, and researchers from the University of Pittsburgh studied the coastal marshes in Aceh Province of Indonesia that were inundated by 115-foot waves. As Reuters reported, "They explored low areas between beach ridges called swales, which are known to trap tsunami sand between layers of peat and other organic matter, and discovered a layer of sand beneath the most recent layer, from 2004, that was from an event that occurred 600 to 700 years ago."

Chulalongkorn University's Kruawun Jankaew told Reuters, "Tsunamis are something we never experienced before, and after 2004, people thought it was something we would never experience again. But from this, we are able to identify that the place has been hit by a mega-tsunami in the past. So even though it is infrequent for this part of the world, it still happens and there is a need to promote tsunami education for coastal peoples."

Wise words from a wise woman. If nature is always on the move, knowing when, why, how, and where it is going is more than a matter of intense interest, it can be a matter of survival.

CHAPTER 5

HEEDING NATURE'S CLOCK

On May 23, 2007, there was a gathering of middle-aged men in the back room of the New York Botanical Gardens library to celebrate the 300th birthday of the Swedish naturalist Carl Linnaeus. Although there was no cake with candles, according to James Barron's account of the event in the *New York Times*, the gathering itself was a tribute to the man who is considered the father of systematic botany. Both physician and botanist, Linnaeus served as a naval surgeon, taught at Uppsala University, and wrote 180 scholarly works. Instead of lifting glasses in tribute to Linnaeus, the New York celebrants passed around and discussed some of these volumes in their collection.

Wanting to liven things up a bit, Robbin C. Moran, curator of ferns and the library's Linnaeus expert, reminded the gathering that he caused a scandal in his own time by creating what was regarded as "botanical pornography." As a twenty-two-year-old university student, Linnaeus turned the usually bland New Year's Day paper required of university students into a "bombshell" by declaring that "every animal feels the sexual urge" and added in his paper, "Yes, love comes even to the plants." When he went on to classify plants as brides and bridegrooms, this form of sexual classification was considered too immodest to teach to women and children. A German critic named Johann Siegesbeck accused Linnaeus of producing "loathsome harlotry" and asked, "Who would have thought that bluebells, lilies, and onions could be up to such immorality?" Linnaeus got even by naming a noxious weed Siegesbeck.

Linnaeus was a public relations genius before the term was invented. He undoubtedly used forbidden discussion of sex, the strongest human urge, to shock people into being aware of the vitality that he found in all forms of life. He was known as an attention getter, and this was affirmed by his playful creation of the "flower clock."

In the northern hemisphere some flowers open at certain times during the twelve daylight hours of summer. Drawing upon his close observation of plant life, Linnaeus laid out a clock-faced garden in which he would display the time through blooms within a half hour's accuracy. Starting a 6 A.M. with the opening of spotted cat's ear (*Hypochoeris maculate*) the clock ran as follows: 7 A.M.—African marigold (*Tagetes erecta*) opens; 8 A.M.—mouse-ear hawkweed (*Hieracrum pilosella*) opens; 9 A.M.—Prickly sowhistle (*Sanchus apser*) closes; 10 A.M.—common nipplewort (*Lapsana communis*) closes; 11 A.M.—Star of Bethlehem (*Ornithogalum umbellatum*) opens; 12 noon—passion flower (*Plassiflora caerulea*) opens; 1 P.M. childing pink (*Dianthus sp*) closes; 2 P.M.—scarlet pimpernel (*Anagallis arvensis*) closes; 3 P.M.—hawkbit

(*Leontodon hispidus*) closes; 4 P.M.—bindweed (*Convolvulus arvensis*) closes; 5 P.M.—white water-lily (*Nymphaea alba*) closes; 6 P.M.—evening primrose (*Oethera crythrosepala*) opens.

In this way, Linnaeus managed to stage a stunning demonstration of the daily rhythms to be found in all forms of life on Earth, human beings included. These cycles are as reliable and predictable as the celestial orbits from which they take their cues. Insects, birds, animals, and people may not put on as precise and visible a show of the rhythms animating them as Linnaeus's flowers, but they all march to the same drumbeat of light. Although there are many cycles of light and time affecting life, the twenty-four-hour cycle of night and day is the most basic. In the parlance of botany and biology, rhythms of this cycle are called *circadian* from the Latin for "about a day."

The study of natural cycles within living things is one of the more rapidly developing sciences of our time. Using the Greek word for time, scientists have a new term—*chronobiology*—for the new branch of an old discipline. The intricacies of what could be called the biological clock and the challenges they present to researchers tinkering with it can be judged from a statement by John Burns, a chronobiologist who once headed the Foundation for the Study of Cycles: "About one hundred new biological cycles are described every day, and this makes it humanly impossible to keep track of them all." Nevertheless, chronobiologists are encouraged by what they have been able to glean from their reading of the biological clock, and they are able to give sound scientific advice on how to improve life in matters as diverse as acquiring a better understanding of physical and psychological feelings, organizing work more productively, improving agricultural output, sleeping more soundly, dispensing medicine more effectively, and getting over jet lag. Although Dr. Burns told me with scientific caution that "biological clocks aren't really understood yet," the wealth of new material being mined through research is a guarantee of more revelations to come.

An International Society for Chronobiology with hundreds of members is, by its very existence and geographical spread, indicative of the range and growth of the discipline. A glance at only a few of the abstracts of some 213 papers presented at the Nineteenth International Conference in Maryland in June 1989 and published in its house organ, *Chronobiology,* shows the scope and variety of research in progress and its relevance to the human condition:

- A study group in France looked into "rhythms of stimulated gastric acid secretion in duodenal ulcer" and concluded that there was a four-month ultrannual (less than a year) rhythm involved.
- A University of Texas School of Public Health report on "circannual variation of human mortality in Texas" found that "a six-month period was detected in ischemic heart disease mortality with peaks in January and July. Suicides, in contrast, were most common around May. The etiology of seasonal patterns of human mortality is as yet undetermined: it could involve seasonal variation in environmental conditions as well as circannual rhythms in physiology and behavior."
- A West German investigation of "melatonin treatment of jet lag" came up with what may be good news for world travelers: "In general the results indicate that melatonin [a secretion of the pineal gland that acts as a natural relaxing agent] may be an effective zeitgeber [a common chronobiological term, from the German for 'time giver' which means an agent that

initiates biological rhythm] for human subjects. Consequently melatonin may be used to influence the circadian system after time zone transitions to reduce jet lag symptoms."

- Clinical experiments in timing dosages of cancer drugs in circadian rhythms resulted in a report that stated emphatically: "Living organisms are not 'zero-order' in their requirements for a response to drugs. They are predictably resonating dynamic systems which require different amounts of drugs at different times in order to maximize desired and minimize undesired effects."

- An Italian group made a systematic study of digestive disturbances in shift workers as compared to nonshift workers and expressed the conviction that "shift work is *per se* responsible for digestive diseases in the workers engaged in it" and that "it is very important to diminish the kind of shift work which may produce environmental, psychological, and motivational differences."

- Authors from the Department of Plant Biology, University of Minnesota, Department of Agronomy, University of Wisconsin, and the Agricultural Research Service of the U.S. Department of Agriculture joined in an overview that said: "An awareness of biological oscillations and attempts to understand these phenomena are important to increasing the productivity and efficiency of agriculture, the quality of agricultural products, and environmental quality. The utilization of biological oscillations by manipulating or taking advantage of their characteristics will become increasingly important in animal and plant strategies."

That some of these studies have continued and expanded is apparent from an announcement on the 2009 Web site of the International Society for Chronobiology. Following up on the Italian concern about the deleterious effects of shift work on health, a working group of the International Agency for Research on Cancer, affiliated with the World Health Organization, had come up with the statement that "shift work that involves circadian disruption is probably carcinogenic in humans." Whether the "probably" can be taken out of that sentence remains to be seen, but the fact of such ongoing international cooperation to deal with problems common to all is one of the most rewarding discoveries in our tour through cycleland.

There is reliable consensus among chronobiologists, cycle scholars, and others concerned with the interlocking rhythms of the universe and terrestrial organisms that both the quality and quantity of life can be enhanced by paying more attention to what is already known for sure about the biological clock. There are a number of truisms in this area that are beyond debate. One of them is that human beings are by nature diurnal animals, which means that they come to life during daylight hours and sleep during the night—a cycle that rolls in reverse for nocturnal creatures such as bats. It is possible for human beings to function by night and for bats to fly by day, but either effort is contrary to the clock. Fortunately, living organisms are astonishingly adaptable to changing circumstances, but adaptation to unnatural conditions almost always exacts a price, as noted in the research on shift workers. With respect to the humans at least, this price has been largely unmeasured during the short century or so since an explosion in technology gave people what seemed to be the means to bend nature to our will. In that perspective, the new knowledge coming out of chronobiology can be seen as a paradox. On the one hand, it has revealed the high price of resisting the driving cycles of nature; on the other hand, it has suggested ways to compensate, as noted in the German research on using melatonin to deal with jet lag.

Central to the fact that biological clocks are not "really understood," according to Dr. Burns, is the mystery as to how their oscillations or cycles are produced. "Some people think that they are produced inside the organism and some from outside," he said, and so far there is good evidence to support either, or both, of these views. A lot of this evidence is accumulating in studies of the effect of light.

Consider some causes for confusion. Seasonal cycles, in which the major factors are duration and warmth of sunlight caused by the tilt of the Earth with respect to the Sun, are self-evident in the migrations and matings of the animal kingdom, and germination and flowering among the plants. This has led to logical postulations. Small mammals, such as the hare and ferret, are called long-day breeders because the lengthening of days at the end of winter seems to result in mating that will produce young by spring. Like the circadian cycle itself, the theory about bats runs in reverse: the earlier twilight of September days that presages longer, livelier nights, is their mating cue. But nature is a signal switcher. For instance, sheep kept under constant light for some three years went right on breeding in the same old cycle, giving rise to the distinct possibility of an endogenous sexual rhythm. An even more thought-provoking indication that living things have a built-in circannual clock is seen in the fact that European trees transplanted by nineteenth-century colonists to the tropics came into leaf on their northern cycle.

When it comes to human beings, it has been said facetiously that Thomas Edison did away with circadian rhythms by inventing the electric light. If so, he was the right man for the job as he personally scorned wasting time on a night's sleep and made up for the loss by catnapping throughout the day. In any event, there is no doubt that Edison's invention is one of the major devices that gives modern humans the feeling of having gained control over nature. Some recent investigations are supportive of this view. Nobody needs a psychiatrist to diagnose or describe the winter blues that can accompany short, dark days. But in some people they can become a form of clinical depression known as seasonal affective disorder (SAD). This affliction is apparently caused by oversensitivity or overreaction to melatonin, the pineal hormone which is the natural relaxant that flows into the system at dusk to ready the body for sleep. Researchers have discovered that SAD victims exposed to thirty minutes of high daily levels of wide-spectrum illumination are able to shake off the winter blues.

"If we can do with light what we have been trying to do with drugs or motivation, we are vastly better off," Dr. David F. Dinges, a biological psychologist at the Institute of Pennsylvania Hospital told the *New York Times* in commenting on experiments in which human body clocks were reset by artificial light. The work was announced in the journal *Science* by Dr. Charles A. Czeisler of Harvard Medical School and Richard E. Kronauer, a Harvard mathematician. In forty-five laboratory attempts to readjust the biological clocks of fourteen men aged eighteen to twenty-four they achieved "uniform success." As distinct and easily measurable as the ticks of a mantle clock are the circadian biological rhythms that show up in body temperature, hormone levels, and kidney function. To reset the clocks the researchers exposed their subjects to five hours of bright light when their body temperatures were lowest. The result: One application made the circadian rhythm irregular, a second reduced it, and a third restarted the clock the way that dawn lifts the temperature to induce waking.

The ramifications of this research are manifold and have yet to be put to the test. Researchers suggest that this could be tried by anyone who flies across time zones. If, for example, a person arriving in Sydney, Australia, from New York would spend part of the first few days outdoors to absorb the equivalent of the first two doses of light, he or she would find the internal clock reset to local time by dawn of the third day. This contrasts with other research showing that people take up to eight days to reset their body clocks on a westbound flight and eighteen days on an eastbound flight through six time zones. Other possibilities raised by the Harvard work are using light to reset the clocks of shift workers—some 2.2 million Americans alone—who are more prone to accident in the middle of the night when their temperatures are low, and using knowledge of light's effects to help insomniacs who often aggravate their problems by turning on lights to read or drive away the dark.

Over recent years there have been innumerable studies as to how photoperiodism—the effect of alternating periods of light and darkness on living organisms—relates to the rhythms in human beings. In general they keep revealing bodily links with light. Often these experiments on volunteers involve isolation from normal light and time, as in the case of Josy Laures, a Parisian midwife, who spent eighty-eight days in a deep cave with only a dim miner's lamp for light. Cooperating with Dr. Alain Reinberg and his associates, she took her daily temperature and timed her menstrual cycle for a year before and after the experiment. Josy lived a 24.6-hour day, a statistically significant departure from the 24-hour day she lived by the clock above ground; her monthly cycle changed from 29 days to 25.7 days. This last effect was a surprise to Dr. Reinberg, who searched the literature and found studies showing that first menstruation in 600 young girls in northern Germany occurred most frequently in winter, and that girls born blind reached menarche earlier than sighted girls. All this raised the real possibility that dim light, or lack of light, might stimulate reproductive hormones in women. When Josy came out into natural light again, all of her cycles returned to normal.

Regardless of what may turn up in further chronobiological research, enough is now known about circadian rhythms to provide guidance for more effective living within the natural cycle of light and dark. Most importantly, chronobiologists now agree that individual human beings are, to a greater or lesser extent, either "larks" who feel and function better early in the day, or "owls" whose vitality rises as the day goes on. For owls who have been plagued for centuries by the accepted wisdom of Benjamin Franklin's homily, "Early to bed and early to rise makes a man healthy, wealthy, and wise," it must have come as a godsend when science could prove that the lark/owl distinction is not a matter of character; it depends on that measurable ticking of the inner clock. Body temperature declines at night and rises during the day for all of us on a normal schedule, but, according to Dr. Czeisler, the exact timing of the low point and high point within any individual is what separates a lark from an owl. The inner temperature cycle is as much a part of a person's makeup as eye color or fingerprints, and learning how to live with it rather than wish it were different is the way of wisdom.

Without losing sight of individual difference, researchers have been able to discern averages across a broad spectrum of circadian rhythms that enable them to make very practical suggestions for scheduling a day's activities. In evaluating these keep in mind that even extreme early morning people and extreme night people have cycles that are only two hours apart. Low points in everybody's twenty-four-hour day are between 2 A.M. and 4 A.M. and after lunch, or approximately the same time twelve hours later. Sleep is definitely indicated as the appropriate activity for the early morning lag, and the siesta habit in Latin countries would seem to have been grounded in physical realities. From the scientific point of view, the early afternoon low is not attributable to the two-martini lunch or its equivalent in past eras because everybody experiences it.

Paying proper attention to the afternoon letdown can, in fact, be a matter of life or death. In its April 2007 issue, *Reader's Digest* made this point in an article entitled "Asleep at the Wheel." The article opens with an anecdote about an experienced twenty-three-year-old driver who dozed off while driving a stretch of highway at seventy miles an hour, veered to the side, and rolled his pickup down a steep embankment. The time? 2 P.M., just after lunch on a weekday afternoon. This driver survived because the rumble strips on the side of the road awakened him just in time to cling to the steering wheel during five rollovers. But how many other millions of drowsy drivers have been as lucky? According to a study by the Institute of

Medicine, sleepiness plays a major part in 20 percent of serious car crash injuries.

Just as they warn of low times when certain activities should be avoided, biological cycles provide high times for many others. Morning generally—late morning particularly—is best for important mental tasks such as composition, analyzing problems, and engaging in creative meetings. Midafternoon hours, following the postluncheon lag, are best for repetitive tasks such as filing and sorting or those requiring manual skills such as typing or practicing the piano. Late afternoon into early evening is the optimum for sports. One fascinating finding is that all of the senses—taste, sight, hearing, touch, and smell—are at their most acute in the evening which no doubt accounts for the fact that those hours are universally preferred for dining and dalliance. The science of chronobiology is largely concerned with rooting out the causes of these phenomena, but it may be years before enough data has been collected and thoroughly analyzed and any cogent theories are formulated.

In today's so-called advanced civilizations, where time is determined by mechanical or electronic clocks and where electricity has done away with the absolute need for natural light, human beings (much like laboratory animals) are routinely called upon to perform activities that do violence to the inner clock. Take two common instances: an owl is confronted with a very important examination in the very early morning because it is convenient or essential in terms of a school's computerized scheduling; a lark, compelled to work 9 to 5 by the logistics of the marketplace, can only find time to deal with the intellectual challenge of working out his or her income tax in the evening. Fortunately, human history is studded with instances of people "rising to the occasion." While acknowledging that this is the case, chronobiologists advise being aware of the unintended consequences. Performing out of time with your inner clock can cause digestive disturbances, emotional outbursts, loss of appetite, and errors in judgment. If these reactions can be anticipated and their nature understood, they can be accepted with more grace by all concerned.

The power of the rhythms within us is evident in this passage from *The Rhythms of Life*, edited by Edward S. Ayensu and Dr. Philip Whitfield, one of the most comprehensive reports on current biological research: "It is a basic assumption that circadian rhythmicity evolved in step with primitive life, and hence that it is an essential property of all cells. Certainly single-celled algae and protozoa, that is, the very simplest of plants and animals, have circadian rhythms, and so do isolated culture cells taken from higher plants and animals. . . . The body of an animal or plant, thus, consists of a panoply of clocks at many levels of organization—in cell, tissue, and organ—and in the whole organism that must tick together." But there is a dominant driving clock that dictates overt behavior. It is the part of the organism that responds to light—in the higher animals and human beings, the eye and brain. Animals in the wild instinctively time their behavior in all areas of living from migration to sexual performance to sleep and feeding by this driving clock. Only human beings turn deaf ears to the ticking of this infinitely intricate system of inner clocks, and it is small wonder that great strain results. In this light, an awareness of cycles cries out for a reexamination of our thinking about the nature of time itself.

The extent and nature of suffering imposed upon the human animal by the logical linear, mathematical, economically profitable, man-made measure of time is beyond calculation. There are, however, welcome signs that this form of unnatural servitude to arbitrary time may be coming to an end as a result of more knowledge about the variable, cyclical, dynamic nature of every entity in the universe. These signs range from calls for new scientific and philosophical concepts about time to hard-headed industrial experiments with flextime, instead of the 9 to 5 regimen, to elicit more production and hence more profits out of employees. In *The Third Wave*, futurist Alvin Toffler used signs of new thinking about time as one of his strongest arguments for the thesis that a new form of civilization is in the making.

"Each emerging civilization brings with it not merely changes in how people handle time in daily life but also changes in their mental maps of time," Toffler wrote. He further stated:

> Second Wave civilization, from Newton on, assumed that time ran along a single line from the mists of the past into the most distant future. It pictured time as absolute, uniform throughout all parts of the universe, and independent of matter and space. It assumed that each moment, or chunk of time, was the same as the next. Today, according to science writer John Gibben, "Sober scientists with impeccable academic credentials and years of research and experience calmly inform us that . . . time isn't something that flows inexorably forward at the steady pace indicated by our clocks and calendars, but that it can be warped and distorted in nature, with the end product being different depending on just where you are measuring it from. At the ultimate extreme, super-collapsed objects—black holes—can negate time altogether making it stand still in their vicinity."

Toffler cites Einstein's proof of the relativity of time as a turning point in our understanding its nature. In Einstein's illustration, a man standing beside a railroad track sees two bolts of lightning strike the Earth at the same time—one in front of a high speed train heading north, the other behind it. A passenger in the train sees both bolts of lightning, too, but to his eye they do not strike simultaneously. The one to the north toward which the train is speeding appears to hit first. Thus, the chronology of events—which comes first, second, and so on—depends upon the velocity of the observer. As physics goes beyond Einstein, more questions about the structure of time are raised.

Columbia University's Gerald Feinberg hypothesized the existence of microscopic particles called tachyons for which time moves backward because they move faster than light, according to Toffler, who quoted another physicist Fritjof Capra as saying that time is "flowing at different rates in different parts of the universe."

A different concept of the nature of time would be nothing new in human history. In the Chinese philosophy of Taoism, which dates back to the seventh century before Christ, time was conceived of as cyclical and related to the life cycles of living organisms. This is true, too, of Buddhism with its wheel of life and Hinduism with its recurrent *kalpas* of four thousand million years that comprised a single Brahma day of re-creation, dissolution, and recreation again. Cyclical time predominated in pre-Christian Greek thinking. Pythagoras, for instance, who first heard the "music of the spheres," taught a doctrine of the eternal recurrence of time.

In *Time and Eastern Man,* Joseph Needham presented the argument that the linear view of time is a natural outgrowth of Judeo-Christian thought. "For Christian thought the whole of history was structured around the centre, a temporal midpoint, the historicity of the life of Christ, and extended from the creation through . . . the covenant of Abraham to . . . the messianic millennium and the end of the world," Needham wrote. "In this world-outlook the recurring present was always unique, unrepeatable, decisive, with an open future before it, which could or would be affected by the action of the individual who might assist or hinder the irreversible directedness of the whole . . . The world process, in sum, was a divine drama enacted on a single stage, with no repeat performances."

The extent to which this linear, progressive view of time accounts for the rapid development of modern science in Western civilization is still debatable, according to Needham. Measurable time is an essential dimension in scientific experiments and mathematical calculations, and Needham suggested that the concept of time as linear and infinitely progressive is a psychological spur to scientific striving. "For if the sum of human scientific effort were to be reformed with endless toil aeon after aeon one might as well seek radical escape in religious meditation of Stoic detachment rather than wearing oneself out like a coral-building polyp engaged with its colleagues in blindly constructing a reef on the rim of a live volcano," he argued. Scientists would certainly not be so strongly motivated if they thought that the knowledge system they were building up could perish in some cyclical turn of civilization. It is notable that time in the form of units of duration is essential to today's analysis of cycles. But it is also notable that science's measurement of those units of duration is based entirely on the cycles of Earth with reference to the Sun and other stars.

In the development of cycle theory there is a suggestion that any new concept of time will represent a compromise between these two historical views. There can be no doubt that time as we experience and measure it derives from celestial and biological cycles. But the more these cycles are studied the more apparent it is that they are not fixed. The orbit of the supposedly steady Sun, for example, is now known to vary in response to the gravitational pull of the various planets in their differing alignments. In addition, the shape of a cycle is more likely to be described these days as a spiral—a shape that can accommodate change and progress within recurrence.

The practical importance of how we view time is what we do with it. To acknowledge the relationships through cycles between time, light, and life is to acknowledge the interdependence of all natural systems, an interdependence from which man is not exempt. More flexibility in adapting human plans and enterprises to the reality of time is certainly in order, and the flexibility in thinking about time that Toffler explored is essential to that end. In space, where astronauts see a new day dawning every ninety minutes instead of every twenty-four hours, the current solution to keeping their bodies from getting out of synchrony with environmental time is for them to schedule functions such as eating and resting in accordance with Houston time throughout a flight. There is irony in the promise of freeing human beings from time by experiments in using artificial light to reset the inner time clocks of time defiers such as shift workers, international travelers, and astronauts. If these experiments work, it is simply a confirmation of the power of the cycle of light within the interlocking cycles of time, light, and life rather than any dominance by humans.

One of the deep thinkers about time whose words have stood the test of time is "Ecclesiastes, or the preacher," as the revised standard version of the Bible identifies the author of an Old Testament book. Because he was a poet of cyclical thinking—"What has been is what will be, and what has been done is what will be done, and there is nothing new under the sun"—there is another irony in the preservation of his words within the Hebrew culture which time historian Needham credited with first introducing the linear view of time to world thought. Evidently, it was not possible to exclude Ecclesiastes from the pantheon of prophets, philosophers, and poets, because what he said corresponded so closely with the experience of even unthinking people and because it has yet to be contradicted in any significant way by science. Consider again the words of this preacher:

> a time to be born, and a time to die;
> a time to plant, and a time to pluck up what is planted;
> a time to kill, and a time to heal;
> a time to break down, and a time to build up;
> a time to weep, and a time to laugh:
> a time to mourn, and a time to dance;
> a time to cast away stones, and a time to gather stones together;
> a time to embrace, and a time to refrain from embracing;
> a time to seek, and a time to lose;
> a time to keep, and a time to cast away;
> a time to rend, and a time to sew;
> a time to keep silence, and a time to speak;

a time to love, and a time to hate;
a time for war, and a time for peace.

If he had carried Ecclesiastes's litany into the world of living plants, Linnaeus would certainly have added that there is a time to open and a time to close. Nobody knows yet why this is so, but it would be hard to argue that it isn't so. I am no kind of flower, but I have found that I "open"—at least in alertness and creativity—early in the morning and start closing at about the end of the evening news. Being married to an owl, I have had to summon support for my arguments that my timing is neither peculiar nor the result of some sort of character deficiency from the memoirs of great literary lights who expressed marked preference for working in the morning hours. In researching cycles I have not only discovered hard evidence that these writers were instinctively picking the best hours for mental labor but also that I and my owl, like Linnaeus's flowers, have all along been doing what comes naturally. Thus, in my personal dealings with time, as in so many other matters, knowledge has, as the saying goes, made all the difference.

CHAPTER 6

MAKING THE MOST OF MOODS

"I have a feeling that in spite of all the pain, unpleasantness, and nastiness I have a sweet secret," wrote teenaged Anne Frank in what may be the most celebrated diary of our times. In this sentence, she was not referring to the bloody events of the Nazi invasion of Holland from which she and her family were hiding. She was recording her reaction to the onset of menstruation, so often miscalled "the curse" through much of human history. Nobody would agree more heartily with Anne Frank's welcoming view of her experience than Leslie Botha. A women's health educator and internationally recognized expert on women's hormone cycles by profession, Botha has devoted much of her career to researching and defining the menstrual cycle which she regards as one of nature's greatest gifts not only to women but to all mankind.

Holder of the Edward R. Dewey Award from the Foundation for the Study of Cycles, and member of the Society for Menstrual Cycle Research,

Botha has for years been sounding an alarm against using drugs to suppress this natural hormone cycle that "unites us as women and is the foundation of our being." She tells women by whatever means she can command that "by honoring your hormone cycle you will not only bring sacredness to your life, but you will gain extraordinary power in what you do and how you do it," and adds that "honoring the hormone cycle is also honoring the earth and the lunar cycle."

Botha is far from alone in her stand against unnecessarily tampering with the menstrual cycle. She draws support for her claim to its sacredness and power from historian Rosalind Miles who wrote in *The Women's History of the World* that woman, "with her inexplicable moon rhythms and power of creating new life, was the most sacred mystery of the tribe. So miraculous, so powerful, she had to be more than man, more than human. As primitive man began to think symbolically, there was only one explanation. Woman was the primary symbol, the greatest entity of all, a Goddess." Women were the first to be aware of the relationship between their bodily cycles and those of the Moon and noted this on antler bones as early as 25,000 B.C. Their understanding of the cyclical nature of the universe led them to become the first astronomers, mathematicians, healers, and prophets.

In light of this history, Botha asks the question, "Where has all our power gone?" and answers it in part in an article titled "Health, Healing and Hormones" on her Web site, Holy Hormones Honey—the Greatest Story *Never* Told (http://holyhormones.com):

> Ever since Descartes handed our "souls" over to the church 300
> years ago, and medicine took eminent domain over our "bodies,"

women became crippled. Our hormone cycle is so integral to our sense of spirituality, to our knowingness, intuition, and wisdom. The menstrual cycle was denigrated to a sanctified medical practice known as gynecology, which is nothing more than the intervention and manipulation of the natural hormone cycle.

All of life cycles—from the planets in our solar system to the cellular functions in our bodies. This is a law of nature in our universe—one that must be recognized.

Living with one's hormone cycle is integral to women's health and well-being. Not doing so is a recipe for disaster.

When a woman is able to understand her hormonal changes and how they affect her behaviors—she becomes a powerful entity: a Goddess. She knows when to act and when to reflect . . . when to make changes and when to refrain. She knows when she is most powerful and can move mountains—and when to resonate with what she has accomplished in the last cycle—as well as foreseeing visions of accomplishment in the next cycle.

Living against the normal ebb and flow of our cycling body causes a great deal of exhaustion on all systems that are striving to maintain equilibrium and harmony. I have observed many women in their thirties and forties who look incredibly older than their age—due to chronic fatigue and exhaustion. When the body becomes fatigued, a myriad of pathological problems ensue.

When a woman lives with her hormone cycle she becomes healthy and balanced and in doing so slows aging. Hasn't reversing the aging process been the elixir of the Holy Grail in times past? Our Goddess foremothers did not biologically age as quickly because they lived with the natural ebb and flow of cycles.

Women blame their chronic fatigue on our lifestyles: stress, pressure—juggling families and careers. Albeit these are important factors, the single source of our demise is not honoring the ebb and flow of our hormone cycle. This is the dance of life. This is our dance. And it is a beautiful one.

Botha does not deny that the downside of the cycle can be distressing, that many women experience what is now called premenstrual syndrome or PMS—a dismal mood that can include depression, irritability, anger, and other emotional disturbances that might call for medical intervention. She cites a press release from a biennial conference of the Society for Menstrual Cycle Research: "While we recognize that menstrual suppression may be a useful option for women with severe menstrual cycle problems such as endometriosis, we do not believe that continuous oral contraceptive use should be prescribed to all menstruating women out of a rejection of a normal, healthy menstrual cycle." No woman of Botha's thinking would countenance repressing the natural menstrual cycle simply for personal convenience.

New drugs to suppress the natural cycle keep coming on the market—Norplant, 1990; Depo Provera, 1998; Seasonale, 2003; Implanon, 2008—with the attendant marketing campaigns. They may perform as advertised, but nobody knows what the effect of using them will be in the last third of a woman's life. It will certainly play havoc with what Botha calls "Female Mystique: The Three Phases of Eve" about which she writes:

> It is my theory that before girls enter menarche they are influenced and guided by the fluctuating phases of the lunar cycle. At the onset of menarche and then for the next thirty to forty years, the endocrine system—including the pineal gland that is influenced by circadian rhythms and external influences begins the natural cycle of its own production of reproductive hormones. Once women finish this phase of their life cycle, they enter menopause—and the lunar cycle once again becomes their guide. Living with this natural transition eases the stress of premenstrual tension as well as the hormonal change to menopause. It is only

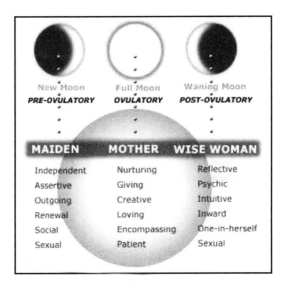

MAIDEN	MOTHER	WISE WOMAN
Independent	Nurturing	Reflective
Assertive	Giving	Psychic
Outgoing	Creative	Intuitive
Renewal	Loving	Inward
Social	Encompassing	One-in-herself
Sexual	Patient	Sexual

in industrialized nations that these two conditions are considered "syndromes" or "disorders" that need to be treated. Women in third world countries are more innately tied to the natural cycles and move through these hormonal changes with ease.

While artificial intervention may be the only way to control the surge of hormones in a woman's body once a month, there is interesting speculation and research that strongly suggests a natural way to control the moods created by that rush. In his book *The Cycling Female: Her Menstrual Rhythm,* published in 1978, Dr. Allen Lien wrote:

The higher centers of the brain have impact on the cycle and can even stop the cycle and prevent ovulation and the menstrual period. This great influence of the brain leads me to speculate about the possibility that the menstrual cycle might someday be brought under the control of the conscious and deliberate will. Such an idea may seem preposterous, but in recent years evidence has been presented to show that such things as heart rate and blood pressure earlier believed to be completely under automatic regulation, may be subject to some willful control. This kind of control is, in fact, under exploration for the treatment of certain types of heart disease. Imagine the importance of discovering a way of willfully preventing LH surge and ovulation and thereby creating anovulatory cycles. Such an idea may sound like science fiction, but knowledge of the menstrual cycle has reached a point where this may be worth thinking about.

That knowledge took a leap forward in 2005 when a team of scientists from Cornell and Rockefeller universities, led by Dr. Emily Stern, used MRI scans to monitor the brain activity of a dozen women for one to five days before their period and eight to twelve days afterward. The women were read words with different emotional connotations—negative, neutral, or positive. The women were selected because they had no outward menstrual mood changes. During the first period, the time when PMS sets in to create emotional disturbance, the scientists noted increased activity in the middle front part of the brain—the seat of emotional control—and less on the sides. The reverse occurred after menses. Because these women did not suffer mood swings, the scientists concluded that the brain activity in some way compensated for the hormonal surge. According to Botha, if the research bears this out, then science will prove that the hormone changes affecting the brain are part of a natural cycle, and the demeaning myths that surround premenstrual syndrome, premenstrual dysphonic disorder, and menopause can finally be laid to rest. What will be understood is that these "syndromes" widely known as "illnesses," are hormonal imbalances that are treatable without the use of menstrual suppressants, antidepressants, and invasive surgeries.

Although much more research of this kind, including observation of the brains in women who do have PMS, is needed, it could be that an attitude such as Anne Frank's is the cause of the compensating brain activity. If so, "the curse" may no longer be part of our language.

There are other hormonal imbalances more widespread and lethal than PMS. In December 1988 the *New York Times* published a remarkable article by William Styron, author of several best-selling novels, including *Sophie's Choice* and *Confessions of Nat Turner*. Styron was explaining and defending the action of an Italian writer, Primo Levi, who had committed suicide by jumping down a stairwell the year before. Other commentators had expressed disillusion and disappointment that a man who had survived Auschwitz and written inspiringly about it could kill himself, as if the act represented a form of moral failure. Styron argued that Levi was a victim of clinical depression, an illness as real and painful as a heart attack. Styron's argument was unusually convincing because it was based on personal confession.

Just a year before Levi's death Styron had committed himself to a mental hospital in order to keep from killing himself. His graphic description of the torture that drove him to this decision bears repeating:

> The pain of depression from which I had suffered for more than five months had become intolerable. I never attempted suicide, but the possibility had become more real and the desire more greedy as each wintry day passed and the illness became more smotheringly intense. What had begun that summer as an off-and-on malaise and a vague spooky restlessness had gained gradual momentum until my nights were without sleep and my days were pervaded by a gray drizzle of unrelenting horror.

In depression, a kind of biochemical meltdown, it is the brain as well as the mind that becomes ill—as ill as any other besieged organ. The sick brain plays evil tricks on its inhabiting spirit. Slowly overwhelmed by the struggle, the intellect blurs into stupidity. All capacity for pleasure disappears, and despair maintains a merciless daily drumming.

The smallest commonplace of domestic life, so amiable to the healthy mind, lacerates like a blade. Thus, mysteriously, in ways difficult to accept by those who have never suffered it, depression comes to resemble physical anguish.

Most physical distress yields to some analgesia—not so depression. Psychotherapy is of little use to the profoundly depressed, and antidepressants are, to put it generously, unreliable. Even the soothing balm of sleep usually disappears. And so, because there is no respite at all, it is entirely natural that the victim begins to think ceaselessly of oblivion.

Styron's words make chillingly vivid the individual agony involved in mental disorder, one of the most pervasive afflictions of human beings worldwide. Consider this doleful drumbeat of statistics issued by the National Institutes of Mental Health in the same year that Styron was stricken:

- In any six-month period, approximately 29.4 million adult Americans (18.7 percent of the population) suffer from some form of mental disorder.
- Between 1958 and 1982, a total of 587,821 persons in the United States ended their own lives by self-inflicted injuries.
- For men, the most frequent disorders are alcohol abuse/dependence, phobia, drug abuse/dependence, and dysthymia (abnormal condition of the mind).

- For women, the most frequent disorders are phobia, major depressive episode without grief, dysthymia, and obsessive-compulsive disorders.

In view of the massive individual and collective suffering caused by mental disorders, it would seem necessary to take seriously any theory that can throw light on the functioning of the complicated human psychological system. In the case of clinical depression, for instance, Styron reported that the cause remains a puzzle despite modern medical advances. There is a confusing mix of probable factors—chemical, genetic, environmental, psychological. With no sure cause, there is no sure cure. But Styron sounded a note of hope with respect to clinical depression that could have come straight out of cycle literature: "Depression's saving grace (perhaps its only one) is that the illness seems to be self-limiting. Time is the real healer and with or without treatment the sufferer usually gets well."

It was the promise that cycle theory offers for dealing effectively with both normal and pathological mental states that led Dr. Jeffrey Horovitz, a practicing psychiatrist, into the surprising career change that made him an executive director of the Foundation for the Study of Cycles. While he was an in-hospital resident in Florida, Dr. Horovitz became intrigued by a rhythm he detected in psychiatric admissions. At first it was a casual observation. When he could not find a bed for a patient he would call another hospital and ask, "Do you have any room left over there?" More often than not, they would say, "No, we're packed here, too." Within a week, the other hospital would call back and report, "We have plenty of beds open now. Do you need any?" By then, Dr. Horovitz's hospital would also have beds to spare. Keeping tabs on such incidents, he discovered that there would be a day or two of massive admissions to all the psychiatric facilities in the city every three to nine weeks. In addition, he observed that more than 50 percent of admissions were recurring—patients who had been hospitalized before.

Like many a thinker who wanders off on a new trail, Dr. Horovitz had a lonely time of it for a while. Whenever he broached the subject of these admissions patterns to medical colleagues, the response was, "Sure there are big days, but so what?" A man who enjoys sharing his enthusiasm, Dr. Horovitz talked to patients about it, too. One of them, an economics professor, brought in a pamphlet from the Foundation for the Study Cycles, and said, "I thought you might find this interesting about recurring patterns in human behavior." Even then Dr. Horovitz let the pamphlet gather dust as there seemed to be no connection between the money markets and medicine. But he picked it up when he became interested in investing and began discussing cycles with brokers. When one of them suggested that there was a correlation between cycles in solar activity and those in the market, Dr. Horovitz had a wild thought: Would the patterns in psychiatric admissions that he was toying with look anything like stock market or solar cycles?

Dr. Horovitz first tried comparing a graph of solar activity with his own of hospital admissions. There was enough of a fit to be interesting, but the real eureka moment came when he picked up the *Wall Street Journal* and saw that a chart of the ups and downs on the market looked very much like that of hospital admissions. He rushed to the office of a medical professor who had been skeptical about his interest in admissions patterns but who was a keen follower of the market. Handing the professor a graph, Dr.Horovitz asked, "What does that look like?"

"It looks like the Dow Jones average over the past three or four months," the professor replied.

"It is solar activity adjusted to try to forecast psychiatric admissions," Dr. Horovitz said.

"What?!"

Although he did not become an instant convert, the professor was astounded and enthralled. Dr. Horovitz's initial results provided only a peek into what might be a world-wide human response to solar activity and its effect on neurological functioning of all animal life on Earth. He now admits that his chart could have been a case of coincidence, but nevertheless the spark it struck turned into flame. "I actually had tears in my eyes when I thought it was working," he recalls. "There was a peek at the connection between human behavior in the financial market and in mental facilities."

So instead of being discouraged, Dr. Horovitz sold his practice and traveled the country with wife and baby in tow to look into cycles. He ended up in Pittsburgh, where the Foundation was then located, signed on to work there, and eventually replaced John T. Burns as executive director. Burns, a chronobiologist, wanted to return to Bethany College, where he continued as secretary of the Foundation's board of directors. Like Dr. Horovitz, Burns was primarily interested in cycles in living creatures and a firm believer in the important role they play. For Dr. Horovitz presiding over what he called the rebirth of the Foundation in Irvine, California, was "a fairy tale come true." But he resigned as executive director in 1989 mainly to pursue, in conjunction with the Foundation, a study he launched to collect worldwide data on the cycles in mental health.

Along with a business he started to help investors apply cyclical knowledge in the markets, Dr. Horovitz has continued collecting data worldwide. His conviction is that, once there is enough data to establish the cyclical nature of mental illnesses, much hospitalization can be avoided. "For instance, if we knew one of those waves of admissions is coming up at a certain time, doctors could tell their patients to increase their medication to a therapeutic dose—perhaps double—to stabilize them through the stress period," he said.

Although work was stalled on what might be called the mass aspects of mental health, the Foundation's files are stuffed with fascinating material on studies over the last sixty-odd years that show cycles at work in the individual psyche. The existence, if not the cause, of cycles in normal mood swings as well as in pathological states has been well established. Much of the work in this area is done by chronobiologists, specialists in the effect of time on living systems. In an overview of this field Susan Perry and Jim Dawson, in their book, *The Secrets Our Body Clocks Reveal,* reported discoveries about clinical depression that illuminate Styron's experience:

> Clinical depression—a severe mood disorder that is typified by intense feelings of sadness and often accompanied by serious disturbances in normal body functions—is also a recurrent illness.
>
> Sometimes the cycles of clinical depression are short and, thus, easy to spot. This is especially true of manic-depressive psychosis, a type of mental illness in which depressive episodes alternate with periods of mania or excessive excitement, hyperac-

tivity, and rapidly changing thoughts. For example, several cases of people with forty-eight-hour manic-depressive cycles (episodes of depression and mania falling on alternate days) have been reported in the medical literature. In one famous case, a salesman in Washington, D.C., became so morose and apathetic on his depressed days that he was unable to leave his car once he arrived at the offices of his clients. On his "up" days, on the other hand, he was the ideal salesman—loquacious and aggressive. He worked around his illness by making appointments with clients on alternate days. Such short cycles are relatively rare, however. Clinical depression is more often characterized by annual cycles. It is most common in spring. Not surprisingly, spring is also the peak season for suicides. Researchers have found that the circadian (daily) rhythms of depressed people are different from those of nondepressed people. For example:

- Body temperature tends to peak earlier in the day in depressed people than in nondepressed people.
- The daily rise of cortisol [adrenal excretion] begins earlier than usual in depressed people—specifically, early in the evening rather than late at night.
- Levels of thyroid stimulating hormone (TSH), which indirectly affects mood, fall to their lowest point at night rather than in the morning, as is the case in nondepressed people.

All this seems to point to the depressed person's body clock being out of kilter.

The reference to the effect of spring is an acknowledgment of one of the external—or exogenous, as they like to call them in cycleland—influences on mood that is clearly cyclical and so generally accepted as to need no proof of its existence. In fact, Dr. Henry Schneiderman, an internist and pathologist at the University of Connecticut Health Center, told the *New York Times* that the phenomenon known as "spring fever" is a "human diagnosis" rather than a medical diagnosis. Its symptoms, he said, are loss of concentration, wistfulness, failure to focus, restlessness—"an unwillingness to work on assigned tasks with the outbreak of good weather after the passage of confining winter"—and everybody gets it. On the whole, Dr. Schneiderman considered spring fever a natural feeling that people should accommodate as much as possible by changing their schedules, but he added, "If there is a stress present, I think spring fever can exacerbate it. So can cabin fever in the winter and a heat wave in the summer. Anything that takes us from our ordinary patterns of life can exacerbate a psychological problem."

The enormous effect of the great natural cycle of the changing seasons is a factor in every facet of cycle theory and observation. In the matter of moods, it is like a shifting backdrop against which the drama of inner—endogenous—cycles is played out in the individual. These emotional cycles in normal people were first studied scientifically more than seventy years ago by Rex B. Hersey, an assistant professor of industry at the University of Pennsylvania. Hersey was engaged to investigate the effect, if any, that mood swings in workers had on safety in a number of industries. Over a period of twenty-three years, he studied more than 1,000 individuals, 200 of them intensively, in America and Europe. His work is still cited because, oddly, it has not been duplicated. One reason for this neglect may be the logistics involved. In one study, Hersey and his assistants virtually lived with twenty-five men in the plant of a utility company for thirty-six weeks, interviewing each man four times a day to get the necessary quantity of data.

From the point of view of his specific assignment, Hersey's results were decisive. In a sampling of 800 accidents, he discovered that 60 percent of them occurred when the worker was "in a worried, apprehensive, or other low emotional state." For the long term, Hersey's insights into emotional cycles in general are even more valuable. In a summary of his study, he wrote:

> All the male workers studied over long periods showed an "emotional cycle." This means that emotional tone varies not only from time to time during the day but also exhibits longer recurrent fluctuations based on internal physiological functioning rather than external causes. This does not mean that every person or even any person will suffer a severe case of the "blues" at regular intervals. It means rather that there will be a lowering of a person's resistance and his capacity for integration and response which may for any definite "low" merely mean that he is less happy than during the "highs" both preceding and following. How acute the depression experienced in the "low" may be is dependent not only upon the internal condition of the person but also on his relation to his outer environment. These recurrent emotional fluctuations in the workers studied in America averaged about five weeks in length, though it varies with the individual. The cyclical emotional "low" can be expected to cover only about 10 percent of the cycle, i.e., between two and four days in a thirty-five day cycle.

Aside from evidence of the existence and periodicity of cycles, some other surprising and significant insights came out of Hersey's work. Consider these:

- In working out with his subjects a rating scale to describe their emotional states, Hersey concluded that "the most destructive emotion, that which more than all others tends to bring men to an abnormal state, is without doubt worry."

- Although cycles vary as between individuals, an individual's cycle is never more than a week off his average. For instance, a person with a five-week cycle might occasionally have a six- or four-week cycle, but "never, in spite of all the buffets of misfortune, in spite of difficulties at home, in spite of great pleasure and unusual success, does this periodicity depart more than one week either way from its norm."

- Emotional "highs" are characterized by a sense of physical well-being, a drive toward activity, making pleasant plans for the future such as earning more money or buying a new car. "Lows" are characterized by lethargy and a reluctance to tackle any task requiring creative energy. The way to stimulate a person on high is to give him a problem to solve; the same person on low would have difficulty solving the same problem.

- During an emotional high, a man in the study "feels he is more powerful than his environment; he is master of his destiny." Yet, ironically, many men got less actual work accomplished during high periods because their energy and enthusiasm bubbled over into socialization, into sharing their well-being and creative thoughts with fellow workers.

- In their high periods, the men slept less, ate less—and had less sex, despite feeling a stronger sex drive. "This anomaly," Hersey opined, "seems caused by a restlessness at night, which the sex activity tends to quiet, rather than by an energetic force driving the worker on."

Perhaps because they were not part of his assignment, Professor Hersey did not dwell on cycles related to sex. From one bit of research, however, he concluded that mood cycles often run along independently of the menstrual cycle. If a woman's mood cycle is, say, five weeks and her menstrual cycle four weeks, there will be times when happiness will be at its peak to dampen the sometimes negative premenstrual effects. He might have attributed the anomaly in male sexual activity to something other than "restlessness at night" if he had taken into consideration the short cycle of rise and fall in sperm count, peaking for most men every three or four days. Then there is the fact that beards tend to grow most on Sunday and least on Wednesday about which Perry and Dawson theorized that "because beard growth seems to be triggered by testosterone levels (which rise during sexual activity), this weekly increase and decrease in beard growth may be the result of increased sexual activity on the weekend."

So far it has proved difficult to subject mood cycles to the same sort of statistical verification and widespread practical adaptations that are possible with, say, economic cycles. They elude what is generally accepted as "scientific" measurement for a variety of reasons. Moods are by nature subjective and hard to describe in exact and broadly applicable terms. The only laboratory in which moods can be examined is the human psyche, and few people are willing to undergo the rigors necessary to arrive at reliable data. The exercise requires testing and recording emotional states on a daily basis over a long period of time in a manner analogous to keeping watch on bodily temperature. A few interested and determined individuals have tried to make laboratories of themselves with results that are more teasing than satisfying.

On January 1, 1959, Jack Dorland, a businessman who served on the board of the Foundation for the Study of Cycles and was founder of his own Society for the Investigation of Recurring Events, embarked on a 1,500-day experiment during which he recorded his emotional state each day before his evening meal. When the graph of his emotional cycle was analyzed, it revealed a seven-day cycle in mood with the high on Wednesday and the low on Sunday. When Nancy B. Brinker reported on the Dorland experiment in the magazine *Cycles* in the early 1970s she opined, "It seems probable that the seven-day week causes or induces the cycle. However, it is possible that the seven-day emotional cycle is universal and that it may have caused the adoption of the seven-day week."

Subsequent research in the field of chronobiology tends to support the latter conclusion. The socially decreed seven-day week, dating from the biblical account of creation, is acknowledged as an exogenous influence on moods. But there is evidence that a seven-day rhythm is stubbornly rooted in biology, in the natural cycles that all living organisms seem to share with the Sun and Moon. A seven-day cycle is roughly one-fourth—a cycle within a cycle—of the monthly lunar cycle. Two experiments in human engineering without regard for nature's structure are worth pondering. After the French Revolution, the nation's new rulers tried to substitute a rational ten-day week for the seven-day week which they thought to have been ordained only by religious superstition. But the French people simply ignored the government decree and continued to take a rest every seven days until the decree was rescinded. More than a century later, not willing to learn from either nature or history, the leaders of the Communist revolution in Russia tried to change the week to five days and then to six before yielding to the people's refusal to abandon their seven-day cycle.

Among others who attempted to reduce mood cycles to usable data was Albert Edward Wiggam, a best-selling popularizer of psychological findings. Wiggam arrived at a personal mood cycle of thirty-six days. He found the knowledge useful: "After you chart your cycle, you will find that you can tell within three or four hours when you are plunging down into a low and when you are about to come up again for air." But John Steinbeck, a Nobel Prize–winning novelist, reported on his own experiment in an exchange of letters with Jack Dorland:

> I read of your mood cycles with interest. Some years ago, I kept a complicated record somewhat similar. Every morning, on going to work I noted such things on a scale from one to ten in several categories: 1) purely physical; 2) mental (alert, dull, inventive, sluggish, etc.); 3) what you might call spiritual (optimistic, pessimistic, pleased, angry, generous, spiteful); 4) relational (by this I meant did I feel close to other people and to my habitat—rejected or rejecting). This was a kind of ecological index.
>
> I kept this record for over a year. Cycles were certainly indicated, but not necessarily parallel. It would be easy to jump to conclusions after such a record, but rather dangerous, because there were not enough hundreds of thousands; and, since I showed the record to no one, the computing machine and the programming agency were the same, namely me. Fortunately, I had no thesis to warp my findings to. An outside diagnosis might have been interesting, but only that.

Although he was not a mathematician or scientist, Steinbeck recognized the need for "enough hundreds of thousands" to arrive at reliable generalizations from individual mood charts. So does Dr. Horovitz. Along with efforts to obtain data from medical institutions, he appealed to individuals to emulate Dorland, Wiggam, and Steinbeck and send the resulting charts to the Foundation for evaluation and inclusion in the data bank.

He devised a do-it-yourself rating system and chart to go along with his appeal and published them in *Cycles*. Using the blank chart on pages 126–127 for each month, place a dot in a different color for morning and afternoon or evening of each day in accordance with Dr. Horovitz's proposed rating system as shown in the hypothetical emotional chart for a woman on pages 126–127. In order to get enough repeating highs and lows to produce a statistically reliable curve, Dr. Horovitz advises twice daily entries over a period of at least six months.

Keeping an emotional chart takes stern discipline, and Dr. Horovitz suggested "toothbrush charting"—making entries while you brush your teeth morning and night or perform any other habitual ritual at roughly the same time of day. Using different colors to connect the morning and evening points of the chart will make the cycles easier to see and evaluate. In the space for notes, both endogenous (menstrual period) and exogenous ("I got fired today") forces affecting moods should be entered.

In a bow to Steinbeck's perception, Dr. Horovitz said that, in the act of measuring personal emotional cycles, a person is both guinea pig and scientist and must therefore maintain as much objectivity as possible to get good results. After charting for several months, the way to find cycles is to look for repeating trends, peak to peak, highs, and lows. A cycle exists if the peaks, the highs and lows, are relatively equal. With these cycles established, it should be possible to predict your own emotional weather in advance and thus make the effort rewarding, whether or not you extend it to participating in the Foundation's study. Dr. Horovitz suggested a few of the uses to which your charts can be put:

> From these results you derive the enormous benefits of being able to forecast your feeling trends and cycles, and to prepare for those changes comfortably and intelligently. Not surprisingly, this has a number of ramifications for you and all of the people who interact with you. Couples who are aware of each other's cycles certainly are able to avoid or eliminate those uncomfortable periods that occur all too often. The same goes for employer-employee relations. Business people can use their cycles to improve their judgment and decision making. The potential benefits are broad, indeed.

If the Foundation gets enough data for significant results, it is probable that they will echo Professor Hersey's discoveries. Hersey used on himself the same system that he developed to measure the emotions of thousands of workers. In concluding his report *Emotional Cycles in Men*, he wrote:

> I am able to forecast the general appearance of my own low periods, with advantage to myself. My cycle runs between five-and-a-half and six-and-a-half weeks. During my low period I am in a very critical mood and do not like to be bothered. At such times I enjoy solitude, and employ the time as much as possible in research work or in the laboratory. I refuse to accept engagements where I shall have to talk in such a way that it is a question of giving myself away. During my high period, I enjoy consultation work and activities that require a lot of energy and vitality. Unfortunately I sometimes become too restless to confine myself to a long-continued task requiring careful, minute work. In many ways I have to be more careful of my high period than my low period, or else may be led into trouble.

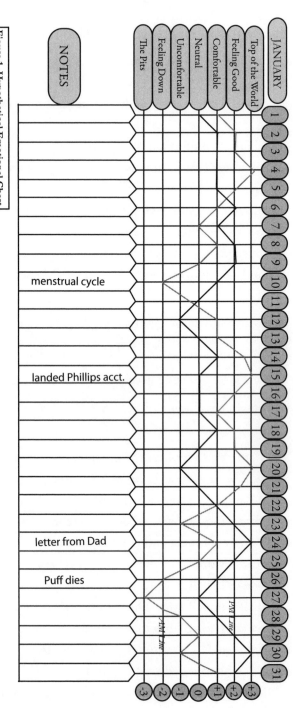

Figure 1. Hypothetical Emotional Chart

Dr. Horovitz's do-it-yourself mood charts: The hypothetical emotional chart he created for a young working woman shows the kind of notes you should make to indicatea outside influences on your moods as, for instance, her high when she gets a bonus on the 20th or her low when Puff dies on the 27th.

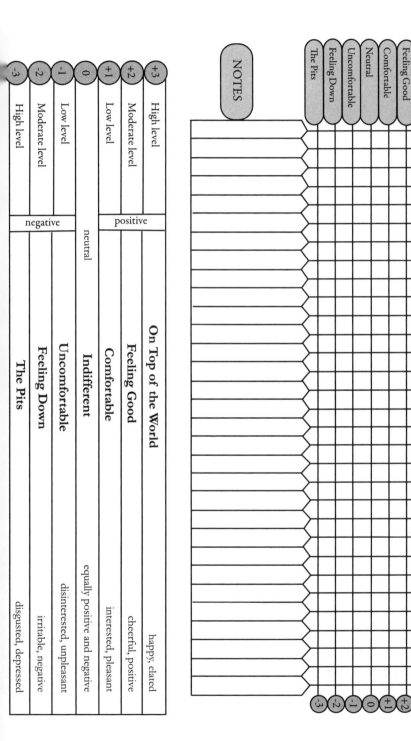

NOTES

	The Pits	Feeling Down	Uncomfortable	Neutral	Comfortable	Feeling Good	Top of the World
1							
2							
3							
4							
5							
6							
7							
8							
9							
10							
11							
12							
13							
14							
15							
16							
17							
18							
19							
20							
21							
22							
23							
24							
25							
26							
27							
28							
29							
30							
31							

+3	High level		positive	happy, elated
+2	Moderate level	**On Top of the World**		cheerful, positive
+1	Low level	**Feeling Good**		interested, pleasant
0		**Comfortable**	neutral	equally positive and negative
-1	Low level	**Indifferent**		disinterested, unpleasant
-2	Moderate level	**Uncomfortable**	negative	irritable, negative
-3	High level	**Feeling Down**		disgusted, depressed
		The Pits		

-3 -2 -1 0 +1 +2 +3

Whether and to what extent a chart of personal emotional cycles might help in instances of pathology such as clinical depression is not yet known. But it does seem probable that becoming aware of the cyclical nature of all life would generate faith in that "saving grace" that William Styron noted. For so-called normal people such as menstruating women who ride a gentler emotional roller coaster, the chart would be a potent reminder that "the pits" are not endlessly deep as well as an antidote to the self-accusatory guilt over feelings of personal inadequacy that so often accompany the downswing of the cycle. The dark holds far fewer terrors when there is light at the end of the tunnel.

CHAPTER 7

CYCLES IN HISTORY

On the morning of the day in 1989 when I planned to put my investigation into the wonderful world of cycles on paper, I did what writers do best on such an occasion. Instead of sitting down to the typewriter—yes, it was that long ago—I brewed a second cup of tea and sat in front of the TV to catch the news, hoping inspiration would come to me. I also rationalized. This was a time of troubles in China, and the latest bulletin about the rapidly changing news in that nation was something a writer could not afford to miss.

My television sprang to life in the middle of the business news. While pictures of foreign nationals crowding the Chinese airports in an effort to flee the country rolled across the screen, an announcer in a clipped British accent delivered a report from London to the effect that British business interests were likely to keep their operations going in China despite the exodus, and despite the government's violation of all international standards of human rights. The reason for this bit of business as usual was summed up by the reporter in a single sentence: "The world economy is now determined by what goes on in the Orient."

I was enthralled. Just the night before in the course of my research I had come across a prediction made nearly forty years earlier by a leading figure in the world of cycles, the late Raymond H. Wheeler: "The next 500 years of history will belong to Asia." The night before that I had interviewed the late Theodor Landscheidt, director of the Schroeter Institute of Research in Cycles of Solar Activity in Nova Scotia who told me that the turbulent events in China were understandable and predictable because they were related to solar cycles.

When I finally went to my typewriter, I sat down not as a somewhat skeptical, though fascinated, reporter but as a beginning believer. Fast forward nearly two decades to what started out as another normal working day—Tuesday, November 7, 2006—that would at last become a true epiphany for me.

Still working as a writer and still dawdling before sitting down to the tool of my trade, by then a computer, I leafed through the *New York Times* while sipping my morning coffee. Without thinking much about it, I noted on page one a story headlined CHINA TO PASS U.N. IN EMISSIONS; on an inside page a feature out of Paris telling me that CHINESE SPEAK THE INTERNATIONAL LANGUAGE OF SHOPPING; and in the sports section a columnist's claim that ASIANS GIVE MAJOR LEAGUES MORE OPTIONS TO CONSIDER. Finished with the coffee and paper, I turned on the computer. It would not respond to my commands. In a mood of frustration and irritation, I dialed its maker's customer service and reached a masculine voice speaking soothingly in a lilt that I recognized from war service in India. Following the voice's instruction, I dismantled the computer. Before he could lead me through putting it together again, I had to hang up to attend to a domestic emergency. When I got back to customer service, a feminine voice with a very different lilt responded, and I had to ask to learn that its owner was in the Philippines. The woman detected the note of ignorance and nervousness about all things mechanical in my voice and wisely instructed me to call a company approved repairman in the next town. When he showed up, I had to deduce the nature of the problem by following his quick and expert hands as he worked; I could hardly understand his Latin American–accented speech.

When the irritations of that day wore off, I began to realize that it was one of those blessings in disguise. I was quite concretely experiencing an aspect of a future that I had been able to predict twenty years before as a result of my research into the subject of cycles—the economic growth of Asian nations. Arriving at the same conclusion by way of different disciplines, two of my sources—a social historian and a scientist—had seen in the cycles they studied an inevitable shift in the balance of power, wealth and influence from Western to Eastern civilization beginning early this century. In addition, they had predicted years of violent conflict between 2008 and 2012. The way these predictions were coming true inspired me to look again at the subject of cycles with the eyes of a convert and share my conviction with readers in this book.

I confess to being a history buff. Most of my books, whether fiction or non-fiction, have been historical or biographical. The hope is that I and my readers might glean from them valuable information about other human lives in other times that can be applied to our own lives in present and future times. The study of cycles is the study of history. The only way to determine whether a suspected cycle is a real cycle and learn how it functions is to search for its appearance throughout history the way Fergus Wood went back 400 years in his tidal research. The beauty of cycles, because they are natural phenomena, is that their history provides a reliable means of predicting the future.

Although prediction of human activity in future by way of cycles in history may be more complicated and less certain than it is in nature, the record of cycle students in this regard is remarkable.

Few thinkers have the mental energy and courage to tackle the whole of human history in search of an organizing principle. But there is something in the air of cycleland that attracts more than its share of these few. Among them the most intriguing figure is that of Raymond H. Wheeler. Part of his intrigue derives from the fact that Wheeler, who died at sixty-nine in 1961, found himself outside the normal parameters of the academic and publishing establishments. As a result, much of his work remains unknown in the intellectual mainstream. It is still probable that the question, "Who is Raymond Wheeler?" would be greeted with blank expressions and total silence in any gathering of erudite citizens beyond the boundaries of cycleland.

So massive and absorbing were the studies to which Wheeler dedicated himself that he never had time to complete them or to turn them into a final, comprehensive published work. Although he held positions of distinction, he was not the sort of scholarly or popular celebrity that appeals to biographers. When she was managing editor of *Cycles* magazine and working on a profile of Wheeler, Diane Epperson discovered that he "died in the process of getting his data together, and supposedly he asked his wife to burn his material because he wasn't recognized."

Fortunately, Wheeler's papers were not burned. They went instead to a former student, S. Howard Bartley, who had become distinguished research professor in psychology at the University of Memphis, Tennessee. Eventually, Bartley passed them along to a friend, Michael Zahorchak, an executive director of the Foundation for the Study of Cycles, who turned one set of Wheeler notebooks into a volume entitled *Climate: The Key to Understanding Business Cycles*. When Zahorchak died in 1987, the rich lode of Wheeler's research and thought remained with the Foundation. In an introduction to the Zahorchak book, Bartley provided this revealing glimpse into Wheeler: "I knew Dr. Wheeler, for he was one of my university teachers and mentor for my advanced degrees. He was so devoted to this long study, and particularly to the basic philosophy of scientific reasoning, that he seemed too serious at the time. But the value of his insights and endeavors are not surprising to anyone my education has made me aware of."

The route by which Raymond Holder Wheeler arrived at being a "too serious" man began in Berlin, Massachusetts, in 1892. Attracted to the study of psychology, he attended Clark College in Worcester and earned a doctorate from Clark University where he studied under John Wallace Baird, an early leader in the field. In 1915, he became a faculty member at the University of Oregon, but his academic career was soon interrupted by World War I. He left Oregon to act as chief of psychological service at Camp Bowie, Texas, and served on a special committee established by the surgeon general to study intelligence testing. Back at Oregon, Wheeler became director of the psychology laboratory. In 1924, he went to the University of Kansas as chairman of the psychology department, a post he held for twenty-two years. Wheeler moved on from Kansas to Erskine College in South Carolina and then to Babson Institute of Business Administration in Wellesley, Massachusetts, thus completing a personal geographical cycle. While he was at Babson, he also spent summers as chief of staff for climatic research at the Weather Science Foundation in Crystal Lake, Illinois, and published for two years the *Journal of Human Ecology* to provide an outlet for his unorthodox views.

Until 1938 when fascination with the big picture of human affairs seems to have overtaken him, Wheeler followed a fairly conventional academic path. One of the rules for getting anywhere along that road, then as now, is "publish or perish," and the publishing is generally expected to reflect growing expertise in the scholar's discipline. Wheeler's rise through the ranks was notably accompanied by nearly thirty published papers on various aspects of psychology. A proponent of the Gestalt school, according to Epperson, "he was trying to figure out why people were resisting new therapy based on Gestalt theory, and on his own he looked back through history to see that every so many years people tended to go with this theory or that one. From that he came up with the idea of cycles in human behavior, and it mushroomed out."

But it may have been more than that. The Gestalt school takes it's name from a German word that can variously be translated as shape, pattern or structure. It maintains that the whole is greater than—or different from—its parts. The genesis of Gestalt thinking was work on sensory perception by Austrian psychologist Christian von Ehrenfels in the late nineteenth century and it was expanded during Wheeler's time by the German scholars W. Kokle and M. Wertheimer. An example of the Gestalt view of reality with respect to perception is that a major or minor mode in a musical melody is a characteristic of the melody itself and not of its individual notes. Again and again this kind of holistic thinking emerges in the study of cycles, and it is to be presumed that it provided the foundation of Wheeler's desire and ability to find the grand patterns in history.

Wheeler's own description of his mental odyssey, set forth in a speech at the Kansas Academy of Science, coincided with that given by Epperson:

> It began over ten years ago, not as a problem in human ecology but as study of fluctuations in human thought and attitude stumbled upon by accident and confined at first to fluctuations in points of view in the histories of psychology, biology, and philosophy. It seemed hardly explainable that these three subjects fluctuated by chance together from one point of view to its opposite and back again down through history. The problem became even more fascinating when upon an examination of the other sciences it was found that they were varying in the same manner. This coincidence suggested looking still further into the history of human achievement, into art, literature, music, and even into political history.
>
> The same pattern was repeated in so many ways, in so many countries and cultures, in so amazingly a precise and objective manner, that the results seemed almost uncanny. Forthwith a rough curve was drawn of these see-saw movements, actions and reactions, characteristic of entire culture patterns, north and

south, east and west, covering every known country in the world upon which historical information could be obtained.

As uncanny as the emergence of the curve that Wheeler called a cultural cycle was the incident that next enlarged his view. A colleague at the University of Kansas, H. H. Lane, who headed the geology department, looked at Wheeler's curve and remarked casually that it resembled a curve he had seen of California sequoia tree growth. The latter curve was developed by a Andrew E. Douglass who used measurements of the rings in 3,300-year-old trees to chart climatic fluctuations over the millennia. Trees had grown slowly during dry periods and rapidly during wet periods. When Wheeler saw the tree ring curves, he recognized at once that "the peaks and valleys in the culture curve corresponded with the fifty-year smoothed tree-growth curve in a fashion that chance could not possibly explain." Although it seemed obvious that the cycles in human behavior were mirror images of the cycles in nature, Wheeler, as a disciplined scholar, knew that he had simply come upon a proposition in need of proof. He would spend the rest of his life accumulating that proof.

The logistics of the Wheeler effort are nearly as impressive as the results. As an original thinker, Wheeler had no model to follow in accumulating the data necessary to arrive at objective "scientific" conclusions. There was no possibility of examining or measuring his vast subject in the narrow confines of a laboratory (although he did once conduct a controlled experiment on rats to measure the effects of temperature), nor would it be possible for one person to do the job. To get the project under way, Wheeler himself read some 250 volumes of history and, with the help of faculty colleagues, undertook a self-instructed course in climatology, meteorology, and geography. With an overall view of what he needed, he assembled a staff of typists, file clerks, draftsmen, statisticians, and graduate students in various disciplines to collect his data. Over the years, he had 200 assistants, working in groups of about forty at a time. It being the depression era, he was assisted with funds from the National Youth Administration as well as the university.

The task to which Wheeler set himself and his helpers was filling the blank pages of a ledger book made to his order by the World Company of Lawrence, Kansas. Each of the book's 2,000 pages measures eighteen by forty-five inches, and the open book spans seven-and-a-half feet. The pages are ruled into forty-six vertical columns with headings such as History, Mathematics, Medicine/Pharmacy, Music, Inventions, Religion/Church, under which are recorded events and developments during the time period designated in the far left column. Thus, it is possible by just glancing from left to right across the horizontal stretch of the book to see what the human race was doing at any given period. The entries are handwritten in the many individual scripts of the assistants and color-coded red for "warm" or green for "cold" as designated by Wheeler, who determined these to be the major climate cycles of Earth. Over a time period that begins with the geological history of Earth and continues until 1936, there are 700,000 items recorded. Because the availability of data increased, the time period on each two-page spread narrows. The years between 600 B.C. and A.D. 900 are covered in twenty-year bites, for instance, while the years between 1800 and 1936 are one-year segments.

Wheeler's ledger can be viewed as a laboriously handcrafted database. In it a mind-boggling amount of raw data is stored and reorganized into usable form. The Wheeler researchers went through 5,000 literary selections and 10,000 titles in science. They examined more than 50,000 samples of painting, sculpture, architecture, costumes, and other works of art from all the world cultures. Their historical studies encompassed approximately 18,000 battles in civil and international conflicts. Possibly because the money ran out, the ledger ends in 1936, but 1936 represents only the beginning of Wheeler's long struggle to use his "computer" to reshape world history into new patterns that would be logical, predictable, and challenging to some of the most cherished concepts about human life and destiny.

In this overview of cycleland, I can present only a summary—with all the risks attendant upon oversimplification—of the Wheeler findings scattered through unpublished manuscripts, articles, notes, and speeches. Whether everything Wheeler believed will be proved in the final analysis is less important than the scope his work gives to cycles as a system of thought. Compared with cycles in most areas under scrutiny, his cycles were long— 500 and 1,000-year climactic fluctuations. The effect of the cycles he saw is to govern the way people, both as individuals and in the mass, feel, think, and act. He argues persuasively that certain kinds of human attitudes and activities in every facet of life from artistic creativity to war correlate with certain climatic conditions over and over again across the millennia.

Essential to accepting Wheeler's view is an acknowledgment of the various effects that climate can have on human beings. In his writings, he offers much proof for this thesis, from historical anecdotes and statistical analysis to biological and psychological laboratory experiments. The major mood-and-mind-affecting element in climate is temperature. Wheeler's research yielded convincing maps, graphs, charts, and statistics to show that what he calls "dynamic civilization," as defined by the location of the world's major cities and the density of human population, is to be found in belts around both hemispheres with a yearly range of average temperature from forty-seven to fifty-two degrees Fahrenheit and an average daily temperature range of ten to thirty degrees. Areas in these temperature ranges also enjoy a type of rainfall favorable to human activity which Wheeler calls "the cyclonic storm," bringing with it wind, moderate to strong changes in temperature, and moderate to strong changes in barometric pressure. Generally, cooler climates with frequent fluctuations in rainfall and temperature have demonstrably brought out the best in people, according to Wheeler, who cites other witnesses of this phenomenon down through history, beginning with a number of Chinese sages and the great Greek physician Hippocrates.

The reason for this state of affairs is that a temperate climate imparts more energy and vitality to the individual human being than either tropical heat or arctic cold. As one of many proofs, Wheeler cites facts that go against the myth that tropical people are more sexually active and fertile than those in temperate zones. "This is a fallacy due, first, to a misunderstanding of the marriage customs and sexual behavior of tropical peoples, and second, to the fact that tropical people look much younger than they are," he wrote. "Actually, fertility develops later in life in the tropics than in the temperate zones, and many marriages are consummated long before childbearing can begin. The average Philippine girl, for example, begins to menstruate a year and a half later than the average girl in Minnesota, and she will not bear children until she is about twenty-one years of age." These observations are supported by animal experiments, including Wheeler's own with white rats in which he learned that litters born in a room kept at ninety degrees matured ten to fourteen days later than those born in a room at fifty-five degrees.

While I was studying Wheeler's works, I had a curious and convincing demonstration of the palpable biological effect of heat on human energy. In a usually temperate part of the country, we were into the second day of heat in excess of ninety-five degrees. Not unnaturally, my wife, Dorrie, complained that she didn't feel like doing anything and added, "It's the strangest thing, but I have the sensation that my heart is beating too slowly. I just know it, and it's scary." It was scary. I did not have the same sensation but then I was not trying to do anything more strenuous than move my eyes across a page. But minutes after Dorrie told me how she felt, I came across this passage in Wheeler's *Climate: The Key to Understanding Business Cycles* that I rushed out to read aloud to her: "It is one of the provisions of a 'wise' nature that, when temperatures external to the body are high, combustion processes within the body slow down. The heart beats more slowly (heat is generated with each heart beat), breathing becomes more shallow, and one's appetite lessens, causing a reduction in digestive work for the body."

Operating on the premise that climate is destiny, Wheeler used tree rings and human accounts of climate at corresponding times to establish four major conditions that could be correlated with human activity: warm-wet, warm-dry, cold-wet, and cold-dry. "These combinations were found to follow one another more or less regularly in the order named and to repeat themselves in cycles of varying length," he said. "Tree growth, in general, registers these four sequences in a synthetic manner, putting in a maximum during the warm-wet climate phase, a minimum during the subsequent hot drought (usually of lesser duration), a second recovery during the next revival of rainfall while it is turning cold, and another, usually a longer and lower minimum during the cold-dry phase in which both variables, temperature and rainfall, operate against growth."

With the cycles worked out, Wheeler was able to go into his ledger cum computer and come up with significant relationships between weather and human behavior. During warm times, state control prevailed in politics, classical themes in the arts, aristocracy in society, and dogmatism in religion. During cold times, individual freedom dominated the political scene, romanticism was favored in the arts, the proletariat was exulted in society, and personal faith had a religious revival.

One of Wheeler's most important findings was that human social organization swings back and forth between authoritarian and democratic ideas and actions in accordance with the recurring climatic conditions. He illustrates this point with many concrete examples through all the years from 600 B.C. to the time of his writing. Two passages from *Climate: The Key to Understanding Business Cycles* are typical of the kind of argument he makes. The first is in support of his observation that hot drought phases of climate promote a tendency toward social control over the individual, including absolute dictatorship, and it would be hard for anyone with memories of the "dust bowl" years and World War II not to be intrigued by this view:

In 1816, England during a hot drought repealed the Habeas Corpus Act. In Germany liberal ideas were suppressed. In Poland the liberty of the press was completely nullified. Massacres were committed on both sides by the Egyptians and Sudanese. In 1821, the Turks massacred Greeks in Smyrna. This was also a period of commercial depression throughout the world.

The most recent hot drought era occurred in the 1930s when an epidemic of dictatorships broke out all over the world. Of the more than twenty republics organized after World War I, only Czechoslovakia survived. Fanaticism, persecution of minorities, and decadent nationalistic movements along with swings toward socialism and communism became the order of the day. The birth rate declined, health suffered, and economic systems all but collapsed during one of the most severe economic collapses in history.

Cooler periods present a brighter picture. Wheeler identified the most favorable conditions as those during a transition from cold to early warm. They produced what he called the "Golden Ages" of history. One fascinating bit of Wheeler data in this regard: Of fifty-three rulers entitled "The Great" by a consensus of authoritative historical sources, 91.7 percent reigned during one of these climatic periods. But the following passage from his book gives a more general picture of the contrast in social organization during cold periods with that in warm ones:

In the cold 1640s, the first written constitution of modern times was drawn up during the war between Parliament and the Crown in the time of Cromwell. Later, during a short cold period in the 1680s, the British Bill of Rights was signed. At about the same time in the colonies, the Quakers of Pennsylvania voluntarily emancipated their Negro slaves.

During the cold decades of the eighteenth century, labor troubles developed almost everywhere. In one of the first strikes in history, bakers and journeymen left their work in protest for higher wages in New York. They were arrested, tried and convicted, but there is no record that they were sentenced. Slave riots developed at the same time in New York and New Jersey. The American Revolution was paralleled throughout the world. In France, the third estate usurped power in the National Assembly on behalf of the common people. Egypt declared herself independent of the Turks, while Austria abolished serfdom.

In Wheeler's understanding of cycles, there are cycles within cycles, all in harmonic relationship with each other. His longest cycle is 1,000 years, and we are now just beyond the middle of the third of these cycles for which he accumulated data. The next harmonic is the 500-year cycle. Both of these cycles are not only cycles in long-range weather trends but in human affairs because at their turning points there is always, according to Wheeler, "the decline and fall of civilizations the world over and the birth of a new era." Each turning point occurred during an exceptionally cold period. As of this writing, Earth is again in transition to a cold period, and we have already passed Wheeler's predicted turning point—the year 2000.

Because cold produces creativity and individualism among human beings, Wheeler cheerfully predicted a renaissance and "a finer and greater democracy than the world has yet known." I am sure that the election of people's candidates throughout Latin America and even the return of Democrats to power in the United States would be seen by Wheeler as an ongoing fulfillment of his prediction. He also called for a shift in the balance of power and influence from Western to Eastern civilization. This cycle in the

Wheeler analysis is as regular as a sine wave in every other 500-year period in history dominated by East or West. "The next 500 years will belong to Asia," Wheeler stated flatly in 1951. Signs that we are already moving rapidly in that direction are everywhere around us.

Although Wheeler exhibited a wider vision and greater daring in prediction than many others, he does not stand alone in his conviction that human history is controlled by the natural cycles of the universe. Another man who shared his view was a Wheeler contemporary, Ellsworth Huntington, a Yale University geographer. Huntington was better known than Wheeler because he published prolifically. His books were used as geography texts in American schools, and his masterwork, *Mainsprings of Civilization,* is still considered a classic of bold, interdisciplinary thought. In that book, Huntington wrote grandly that "the whole history of life is a record of cycles."

Not surprisingly, Huntington was a friend and collaborator to both Edward R. Dewey, founder of the Foundation for the Study of Cycles, and Raymond Wheeler. Huntington once devoted three weeks to fine-combing a 1,000 page Wheeler manuscript that was never published but which earned from Huntington this encouraging judgment: "I believe you have hold of one of the great contributions of human knowledge." In turn, Wheeler was one of the few people whom Huntington sought out when he wanted criticism of his own manuscript. Huntington recognized the truths in Wheeler's arguments as a result of difficult and sometimes dangerous personal experience. An explorer who trekked the wastes of Central Asia, he came upon evidence of towns and agricultural lands that had been overwhelmed by advancing desert and concluded that the great invasions of Western Europe by Mongol hordes were primarily caused by a cycle in climate that made their homelands unlivable.

In his book, Huntington told the story of a specific cycle's effect in much more recent history to demonstrate how climate can determine human destiny. This cycle was first noted by Sir Francis Bacon who wrote in the seventeenth century: "They say it is observed in the Low Countries, (I know not what part), that in every five and thirty years the same kind and suit of years and weathers come about again; as great frosts, great wet, great drought, warm winters, summers with little heat, and the like, and they call it prime; it is a thing I do rather mention, because, computing backwards, I have found some concurrence." The cycle finally got a name—Bruckner— in the later nineteenth century when a German who analyzed data such as the dates of wheat harvests and wine making, the freezing of rivers and the rise and fall of lakes came up with a cycle of European weather averaging thirty-five years. The swing was from an oceanic climate with wet, cool summers and mild, moist winters, to a continental climate of dry, sunny, warm summers and cold, clear winters. It was, according to Huntington, oceanic phases of this Bruckner cycle that caused two of history's greatest migrations—the flight of millions of Irish to America in 1846–48 and again in 1881–91 when the failure of potato crops caused widespread starvation.

One natural cycle that both Wheeler and Huntington consider to be very influential in human affairs is the eleven-year sunspot cycle. This is because the amount of heat or energy the Sun delivers to Earth varies with the number and size of sunspots. Sunspots, which are storms in the Sun's gaseous atmosphere, reach what is known as a maxima on the average of once every eleven years. Occasionally, they are more severe than normal, last as long as two years, and become visible to the human eye. Wheeler claimed that evidence of a correlation between sunspot maxima and the onset of cold climatic phases goes back to A.D. 51 when sunspots and the aurora often associated with them were seen just a year after reports of extreme cold in Britain.

More recently another cycle scholar confirmed and surpassed Wheeler's work in identifying solar activity as one of the keys to history. But the late Theodor Landscheidt, director of the Schroeter Institute for Research in Cycles of Solar Activity, argued that, although sunspots have received great attention because they are so spectacular and well documented, "flares are the most powerful and explosive of all forms of solar eruption and the most important in terrestrial effect." Because flares could not be observed systematically until the invention of the spectrohelioscope in 1926, not enough data has been collected to establish a cycle. But then, as Landscheidt pointed out, it took 200 years to discover the eleven-year sunspot cycle.

Landscheidt had, nevertheless, been able to compare solar eruptions, regardless of flares, with human activity and come up with some conclusions strikingly like those of Wheeler. Claiming that the energy from these solar eruptions which, in turn, are related to planetary cycles, stimulates creativity in human beings, Landscheidt found what he called "borderline phenomena" when an old cycle meshes with a new one. This is a state of instability and change that is characterized by both revolution and renaissance in human affairs.

"When the Sun is very active, as it is now, people are very active," Landscheidt told me. He continued:

> You can see it now in China and Eastern Europe. When the Sun is
> in the eleven-year maximum—and it is there now (1989) or near
> it and will be next year, you get revolutions. Those revolutions
> that were successful were made when the Sun was in the maxi-
> mum. That was true in 1789 with the French Revolution and in
> 1948 when Mao was successful in China. If you didn't observe the
> Sun and looked only at revolutions, you could predict that there
> must be an eleven-year maximum in solar activity. The next maxi-
> mum is coming up, and if you are a revolutionary, I could advise
> you to prepare your revolution for 2002 and be successful in 2004
> or 2005.

And haven't we had revolutionary activity throughout the world in these years? Because Landscheidt also foresaw a period of creativity in which there will be new inventions and new ideas as people come out of a cycle of inertia in 2002, his vision came quite close to that of Wheeler about what would take place during the turning point of a 500-year climatic cycle. And haven't we seen inventions galore, especially in communications, throughout this time? Like Wheeler and Huntington before him, Landscheidt was a serious and disciplined man who was not afraid to make the great leap of looking at creation as a living and interactive whole rather than the sum of indepen- dent parts. I submit that respect must be paid to people like them. When they reached such similar conclusions coming from such dissimilar scholarly disciplines and personal experiences, the odds in favor of their closing in on the truth were highly enhanced. The world according to cycles as they saw it becomes a world in which the shape of events to come is discernable on the mind's horizon.

CHAPTER 8

LOOKING TO THE HEAVENS

The latest news about the universe should be a welcome gift to those who believe cycles play a large role in the scheme of things. While I began writing this chapter, the news came to me as a welcome surprise by way of an article in the *Princeton Alumni Weekly*. Cosmologists at the university are proposing a theory that the universe is cyclical in nature, a fascinating challenge to the prevailing views of both its beginning and its end.

Of necessity, scientific stargazers have to use a lot of intelligent guess-work to arrive at their theories about what they think they see going on in space. There are still as many mysteries as certainties about what is going on up there—or, better, out there. The few things known for sure, according to science writer Mark Alpert, author of the *Alumni Weekly* article are "our universe's size (infinite), shape (flat), and age (13.7 billion years)."

There is, for instance, a force that astronomers have detected and called "dark energy" because they cannot see it. This is thought to be an antigravity force behind the prevailing theory that the universe is inflating—a theory supported by the fact that observers can see the colors of distant objects changing and their size shrinking. The end will come in trillions of years when the expanding universe runs out of hydrogen to produce new stars.

But "dark" remains an appropriate adjective for this energy. As Adam Riess of Johns Hopkins and the Space Telescope Science Institute told the *New York Times*: "If this was a fox hunt and dark energy was the fox, I think they have closed off another escape route. But there is still a lot of terrain left for the fox, and we've seen little more than a glimmer of fur." Such skepticism may have led Princeton's Paul Steinhardt, one of the original proponents of the inflation theory, to change his mind and come up with a cyclical version of the universe's beginning and end.

"In 2001, [Steinhardt] and Neil Turok of Cambridge University published their first paper of an alternative to inflation called the ekpyrotic model (*Ekpyrosis* is the Greek word for conflagration)," Mark Alpert reported in his *Weekly* article:

> The model was inspired by string theory, which posits that the fundamental particles and forces actually are minuscule strings vibrating in extra dimensions of space that we can't perceive. In one variant of the theory, most of the strings in our universe are attached to a three-dimensional boundary called a brane. Although these strings are stuck to the branelike magnets on a refrigerator, the brane itself can travel through the extra dimensions.
>
> But gravity also can extend into the extra dimensions, which raises the possibility that one brane could attract another. When

Steinhardt and Turok considered what would happen if another brane collided with ours, they found that the impact would infuse our universe with energy and force it to expand—an event that looks very much like the Big Bang. And because the branes would ripple slightly as they approached each other, the collision would produce the small fluctuations in density observed in the CMB [cosmic microwave background] studies.

Better yet, Steinhardt and Turok later realized that their alternative hypothesis also can explain cosmic acceleration. After the collision the branes would bounce apart, but they will still be gravitationally attracted to each other, and this attraction would speed up the expansion of our universe. Eventually the branes would stop moving apart and hurtle toward each other again, causing a slow contraction of our universe and finally another Big Bang. Then the cycle would repeat indefinitely, with the branes clashing like a pair of cymbals. This updated version of the hypothesis, which was renamed the cyclic model, is quite different from the earlier idea of the Big Crunch, in which the universe would collapse under the force of its own gravity. In the cyclic model, the matter of our universe doesn't re-concentrate; rather, the gravitational field between the branes periodically pumps new energy into our cosmos.

All this would happen, if it happens at all, in many millions or trillions of years. Meanwhile, the stars that human beings can see do move in quite evident cycles and have a lot to tell us about our lives on Earth. Indeed, a modern cycles theorist, Ray Tomes, claims that "the universe, believe it or not, is nothing other than a giant musical instrument with a very special

but predictable pattern of harmonically related oscillations which determine
the structure of everything from galactic clusters to subatomic particles. Although this theory is properly called the Harmonics theory it may be alter-
natively known as the Big Bong theory! The single axiom of the Harmonics
theory is that . . . the universe consists of a wave which develops harmonics
and each of these waves does the same." Although in tune with the rather
recent discoveries of physics, Tomes's theory might be called a harmonic of
one proposed by a Greek philosopher in the century before Christ.

The man's name was Pythagoras, and he is credited with first claiming that the heavenly bodies make music. He, or at least his followers who
were known as the Pythagorean school, meant this quite literally, and their
reasoning was based on the fact that they had discovered what is now called
harmonics. In those days thinkers about the workings of the universe did
not have the tunnel vision that too often results these days from the separation of modern science into different and sometimes competitive disciplines. Thus, Pythagoras was a farsighted pioneer in both mathematics and
astronomy, and the areas of thought he opened up still have an important
place in cycle theory.

Astronomy may well be the oldest of the sciences, and it certainly reveals some of the most basic and prevailing cycles in science. Cycles and
overlapping or interacting systems of cycles are to be found everywhere in
astronomy, from the movement of the solar system through the galaxy to the
orbits of the planets to the recurrence of sunspots.

There is ample evidence that human beings in prehistoric societies made
practical use of their observation of the heavens for telling time, navigating,

and planting crops. Many of them made valiant efforts to understand and measure their observations. One theory about the curious construction of massive sandstone blocks in England known as Stonehenge is that it is an astronomical calculating device because its inner ovoid points to the place on the horizon where the Sun rose on Midsummer Day in 1680 B.C. In his classic *Conquest of Peru*, historian William H. Prescott noted of the Incas:

> In astronomy they appear to have made but moderate proficiency. As their lunar year would necessarily fall short of the true time, they rectified their calendar by solar observations made by means of a number of cylindrical columns raised on the high lands around Cuzco, which served them for taking azimuths, and by measuring their shadows they ascertained the exact times of the solstices. The period of the equinoxes they determined with the help of a solitary pillar, or gnomon, placed in the center of a circle, which was described in the area of the great temple and traversed by a diameter that was drawn from east to west. When the shadows were scarcely visible under the noontide rays of the sun, they said "the god sat with all his light upon the column." Quinto [sic], which lay immediately under the equator, where the vertical rays of the sun threw no shadow at noon, was held in especial veneration as the favored abode of the great deity.

As in this instance, religion and astronomy have always been closely associated. For the sake of survival, human beings have had to be aware of the forces exerted upon them and their environment by the Sun and the Moon and the stars. Not only were these forces for the most part an unfathomable and uncontrollable mystery of vital importance to every individual but the heavens in which they moved were also a source of awesome beauty.

Historically religion served humans as a device for coping with mystery and awe, and the Inca meld of worship and calculation was typical. Unfortunately, religion has also historically acted as a brake on new discovery and fresh thought. Learning new truth about natural laws generally results in dethroning either the gods or humans, or both. The revelations of Pythagoras are a case in point.

By the time of Pythagoras scholars in China, Egypt, Babylonia, Greece, and probably the Americas had identified recurrent cycles in the movement of heavenly bodies and had crudely charted many of them. It must be assumed that Pythagoras was reasonably well acquainted with the body of knowledge in the so-called civilized world because he moved around physically as well as mentally. Born and educated in Greece, he visited Egypt, which was another center of learning, and later settled in southern Italy where he founded the Pythagorean brotherhood. His contribution to astronomy was to postulate that the Earth was a globe hung freely in space and traveling in a circular motion with all the other heavenly bodies. Previously, Earth was widely held to be a flat disk, stationary with respect to the inferior bodies moving above and across it.

Pythagoras's astronomical insights were brushed aside by his fellow Greeks. Aristotle in the fourth century B.C. and Ptolemaeus in the second century went along with the concept of a stationary Earth at the center of the universe. This was what's called a "homocentric" system, and it dominated Western thought for nearly 2,000 years, partly because it fit so well with Christian theology's view of the universe as created by a personal God for man's enjoyment and dominance. Only when Nicolaus Copernicus, a Polish astronomer of the fifteenth century A.D. came along to describe a system in which a spherical Earth rotated around a spherical Sun did Pythagoras come into his own. But not immediately. Copernicus's "heliocentric" theory was condemned by the Inquisition and his book placed upon the index of prohibited books; both God and humanity were in danger of losing their power. Now, of course, the Copernican system is, in essence, what we still accept to be the astronomical truth.

Pythagorean thinking has been even more influential in creating a mathematical basis for cyclical theory than it was in astronomy. Pythagoras was fascinated with numbers and the way in which they could serve as an abstract expression of concrete occurrences. Indeed, Aristotle said that the Pythagoreans held numbers to be the first things in the whole of nature and the elements of numbers to be the elements of all things. One result of their working with the properties of numbers is a theorem known to every school child today (including the author in *his* day, even though he, like many, shunned the study of mathematics and science): i.e., the square of the hypotenuse of a right-angle triangle is equal to the sum of the squares of the other two sides.

The discovery that set Pythagoras afire and still sheds light was the relationship between the vibrations that can be heard in a plucked, stretched string and their numerical equivalents. Whether in a violin string set to vibrating or in a tuned electrical circuit, there are other vibrations with a frequency—or rate of vibration—that are multiples of the fundamental vibration. They are harmonics or overtones. For example, the first harmonic vibration on a fundamental frequency of 100 cycles per second would be one of 200 cycles per second—what's called an octave in the eight tone musical scale. As a test of his faith in the wonders of numbers, Pythagoras divided a monotone string according to the arithmetical ratios one to two, two to three, three to four, four to five, and five to six. When he plucked it out came consonant overtones. This is analogous to the placement of frets on the neck of stringed instruments such as violins and guitars; by pressing a finger against a fret, the player changes the length of the vibrating string to produce a different tone. In Pythagoras's case, the ratio of two to two produced the octave (C-C in the key of C), two to three—the ratio of the entire string to two thirds of its length—produced the fifth (C-G) and so on. Pythagoras postulated that only ratios of integers up to six produce consonant—i.e., agreeable—harmonics. Although the whole range of harmonics was unknown to him, he was very close to being right. Theorists have since included five to eight which creates a minor sixth, and eight represents the equal sounding octave. The present consensus is that the third, fourth, fifth, and sixth are the consonant intervals.

Because they thought that the heavenly bodies were separated from each other by intervals with the same mathematical ratios as the harmonics in sound, it was logical for the Pythagoreans to think of the spheres as singing. But the Pythagorean brotherhood was involved in what were viewed as less-than-logical beliefs such as the kinship of men and beasts that formed the basis for their vegetarianism, and their heavenly harmony was put down as a form of mysticism that became the property of poets rather than scientists. Shakespeare referred to "music from the spheres" in *Twelfth Night*, and Sir

Thomas Browne wrote that "there is music wherever there is harmony, order, or proportion; and thus far we may maintain the music of the spheres."

Recently, however, a scientist who was a prominent figure in cycle research suggested that the Pytharoreans were hearing something very real—at least insofar as the mathematical and musical harmonies are equated and related. He was Theodor Landscheidt. Like Pythagoras before him, Landscheidt took an interdisciplinary approach to the puzzles presented by the workings of the universe. By dictionary definition, holistic thinkers adhere to "a theory that the determining factors especially in living nature are irreducible wholes," and they abound in cycleland. But Landscheidt's broad background made him unique, even there. Born in Bremen, Germany, he studied philosophy, law, and natural sciences at the University of Göttingen where he earned a doctorate. He entered the legal profession and became a West German high court judge until his retirement. For him, the law was a rational way of making a living, of earning money to establish the Schroeter Institute; his real profession was studying the universe. "I got into cycles to understand what was going on," he told me:

> Physicists tell you that everthing is vibrating. Electrons vibrating around the nuclei and so on and so on. If you find this already in physics at a very basic level, it should emerge at higher levels, too. So I began to look for cycles. When I found some, I got intrigued because it is a possibility to make predictions. I began that research twenty-five years ago. While I was a judge, I was always working in all these fields—astronomy, statistics, psychology, economic cycles, and all that. I needed special mathematics, too, and I got it; I studied it.

When he retired to devote all his time to the study of cycles, Landscheidt moved to Nova Scotia because "Europe was too crowded" and there he wrote an intriguing book, *Sun-Earth-Man*, in which, among many other exciting propositions, he made a new case for heavenly harmony. Computing intervals in the energy wave from the Sun over a period stretching from 5259 B.C. to A.D. 2347, Landscheidt found mathematically consonant intervals equivalent to the major sixth (three to five) and minor sixth (five to eight) in music emerging. Moreover, he reported that a study of growth rings of Bristlecone pine trees in the White Mountains of California dating back to 3431 B.C. shows intervals coinciding with his solar energy chart's consonant intervals with a ratio of five to eight, the minor sixth. In discussing an analysis of the periodic alignment of Jupiter, the Sun's center and the solar system's center of mass, Landscheidt wrote:

> It is intriguing that the ratio of the superimposed harmonics four to five to six is that of the major perfect chord in musical harmony. Kepler [sixteenth-century German astronomer, Johann Kepler] had found just this chord C-E-G when he analyzed ratios of the velocities of different planets at aphelion [most distant from the Sun] and perihelion [nearest the Sun]. Kepler's finding is also valid for the outer planets Uranus to Pluto. Thus, the major perfect chord turns out to be a fundamental structural element of the planetary system. The results presented here are a new substantiation of the Pythagorean harmony of the spheres.

The Pythagorean harmony is apparently there, but so far it has yet to be heard except by the informed mind. Meanwhile, the Copernican concept of a heliocentric solar system comprised of bodies in cyclical motion, has been confrirmed and enlarged upon by observation and experience. Almost daily, new discoveries are made through finer instruments and space exploration, leading to new theories about the universe, and they are often treated as front-page news.

Cycle enthusiasts with a mathematical bent can feel themselves part of this astronomical symphony as they work with their equations and computers. But anyone equipped with a reasonably good eye, a clear night, a spot to stand on with a view near the horizon in all directions, and a dollop of patience can experience a physical sensation of cyclical movement. Looking east, an observer in the middle latitudes of the northern hemisphere would see stars rising and moving to the right at about fifteen degrees an hour; in the west, stars would appear to move right and downward; at the horizon north and south, the stars would move right but neither rise nor fall. Because what the ancients thought was a movement of the heavens is really the spinning of the Earth—at speeds up to a 1,000 miles an hour—the observer will find the movement slowing as the eye travels upward from the northern horizon and stopping entirely in the area of Polaris, the bright North Star, which is only a degree away from the pole. In the southern hemisphere, movements would be in reverse.

With the cycles of heaven so obvious, regular, and influential, it is not surprising that their action is the substance of much of the study and speculation of cycles scholars and analysts. Edward R. Dewey liked to dazzle readers with computations of the great cycles. "You are," he once wrote, "at this moment spinning around at speeds up to 1,000 miles per hour on a ball that is flying at 66,000 miles per hour around a Sun that is traveling 481,000 miles per hour around a Milky Way that is rocketing at 1,350,000 miles per hour around a supercluster of galaxies. And all of this in a pattern of cycles so exact that it is possible to predict our position in the universe a thousand years from today." That pattern results in a cycle of 23 hours, 56 minutes, and 4.09 seconds for Earth's rotation relative to the stars; a cycle of 365.242 days for the Earth's orbit of the Sun; and a cycle of 230 million years for the whole solar system to circle the Milky Way.

Just as there are frequencies within frequencies to create harmonics, there are innumerable cycles within cycles in the starry skies. Many of these have been translated into reliable numerical values that have found increasing use in such matters as the stock market and weather predictions. Francis J. Socey, a Weems, Virginia, professional meteorologist for more than fifty years who earned a living forecasting for almanacs and commodity markets, put great store in the relationships among the planets, the Moon, the Sun, the Earth. The time it takes them to complete their orbits became fixed in Weems's mental computer. Talking to me, he reeled these cycles off from memory—Mercury 88 days, Venus 224.7 days, Mars 687 days, Jupiter 11.86 years, Saturn 29.46 years, Neptune 165 years. Tidal authority Fergus Wood used a composite of 136 representative lunisolar cycles to create a table of the maximized gravitational forces on Earth. Economist A. Bruce Johnson stirred half a dozen planetary cycles into a mix of economic cycles and other data to come up with a foreshadowing of the Dow Jones averages on the stock market.

Typical of a well-established celestial cycle is that of the spots on the Sun. The importance of this phenomenon is, of course, related to the Sun's controlling power in the solar system. Consider a few of the impressive facts about this star:

- It is 93 million miles distant from Earth.
- It has a diameter of 865,000 miles.
- It's mass is approximately 2 billion billion billion tons, and it comprises 99 percent of the solar system's matter.
- It burns this matter at the rate of 4 million tons per second generating temperatures of 6,000 degrees centigrade on the surface and many millions of degrees at the core.
- It rotates in a cycle like the Moon, but not as a solid ball because the period of rotation is only 25 days at the Sun's equator and 31 days at 75 degrees of latitude.

Small wonder that this fiery ball that energizes all life on Earth has been an object of awe and worship. Although the presence of sunspots can be detected with the naked eye, they could not really be seen until the telescope was invented in the seventeenth century. One of the first people to open up the heavens with that instrument was Galileo Galilei who included sunspots among the fresh phenomena he observed. But it wasn't until the early nineteenth century that a German astronomer, Heinrich Schwabe, looking through a two-inch telescope detected a rhythmic pattern—a cycle—in the appearance of sunspots with a frequency of approximately ten years. In a thirty-year analysis of sunspot activity since the year 1527, the Foundation for the Study of Cycles refined Schwabe's calculations to fix the average sunspot cycle at 11.11 years.

The nature of sunspots is not fully understood, but Dewey, who directed the Foundation's study, described them thus:

Sunspots are whirling vortices of cooler, seemingly dark gas that blemish the surface of the Sun. They can appear singly or in groups, but they usually show up in pairs. Their size is immense. One group, which appeared in 1946, covered an area sufficient to swallow over 100 Earths. Sunspots are sometimes accompanied by bright flares spitting thousands of miles into the corona and emitting strong doses of ultraviolet, charged particles, and X-rays. Sunspots usually appear and vanish within a few days but frequently they endure for many months, disappearing from our view with each rotation of the Sun and reappearing again approximately two weeks later. Sunspots are also magnetic, and one of their most mysterious characteristics is that when they are in pairs or small groups they act as if they were the positive and negative poles of huge horseshoe magnets embedded in the Sun. In one cycle the leading spots of each pair or group in the northern hemisphere will have a positive polarity while the leading spots in the southern hemisphere will have a negative polarity. In the next cycle the situation reverses itself and the leading spots in the northern hemisphere will be negative while the leading spots in the southern hemisphere will be positive.

Clearly the sunspots have an effect on the Sun's emission of energy and thus an effect on life on Earth. Because the cycle has been so well established at eleven years, it provides a benchmark against which to measure all sorts of cycles and events. Throughout the development of cycle theory, the sunspot cycle has been attributed as a factor in everything from the ups and downs of the money markets, to changes in weather and emotional states, to wars and revolutions. As Dewey noted drily, "In the past century attempts have been made to link nearly every behavior on this planet to these mysterious eruptions."

If there is nothing new under the Sun, there are some new discoveries about the Sun and its behavior that are changing the course of cyclical theory. The late Rhodes W. Fairbridge, a leading thinker in the field of cycles, was professor of geological sciences at Columbia University and consultant to NASA's Goddard Institute for Space Studies. He and a number of colleagues, such as John E. Sanders and James H. Shirley, came up with what a Fairbridge and Sanders paper called "some aspects of celestial mechanics that we think are significant and that seem to have been either ignored by astronomers or cast in the completely wrong terms of a Sun-centered system."

The mechanics begin with the action of gravity—the force which holds the celestial bodies in orbit and which is determined by the body's mass. Because of the Sun's great mass compared to its satellites, it is commonly thought of as a body at rest in the center of the circling solar system. But the fact is that the Sun is as much a body in motion as any other, and the nature of its motion, according to new thinking, exerts an important influence on solar activity. To describe the motion, Shirley used the analogy of a dumbbell with weighted ends being thrown into the air with a spin. The ends of the dumbbell will spin around each other, one in an irregular path. But traced over the whole flight, the dumbbell's point of balance, or center of mass, will make a regular arc, a parabola. In the solar system, there is a similar center of mass—the barycenter—that orbits the center of the Milky Way around which the Sun loops like one of the weighted ends of the dumbbell. Each orbit takes from ten to twenty years in varying diameters; at times, the Sun can be as far as 1 million miles from the barycenter.

After a study of the Sun's orbit from A.D. 750 to 2050, Fairbridge and Sanders postulate:

> The Sun is forced into an orbit around the center of mass (barycenter) of the solar system because of the changing mass distributions of the planets. Irregularities in the solar orbit generate cycles that have periods ranging from a few years to several hundred years. Much of the solar orbit is a response to the movements of Jupiter and Saturn, which change angular relationships by ninety degrees in just under five years. A fundamental rhythm is the Saturn-Jupiter-Lap cycle of 19.859 earth years. Solar-planetary-lunar dynamic relationships form a new basis for understanding cyclic solar forcing functions on Earth's climate.

Landscheidt was also convinced that the planets have a lot to do with the Sun's orbit and rate of rotation and, in turn, its output of energy. Significantly, it was the analysis of one alignment of Jupiter, the center of mass and the Sun's center over a period of time, in which he found the harmonics of the major perfect chord. This sort of detection and analysis of heavenly cycles is a new direction in the understanding of the universe that offers great promise for predicting, if not controlling, celestial forces. It might be either a comfort or a disappointment to people with apocalyptic vision to learn that the more cycles are comprehended the more they seem to confirm the insights and intuitions of the Pythagoreans and poets.

In the seventeenth century, poet John Dryden included uncannily prophetic lines in "A Song for Saint Cecilia's Day":

From harmony, from heavenly harmony,
This universal frame began;
From harmony to harmony
Through all the compass of the notes it rang
The diapason closing full in Man.

CHAPTER 9

THINKING OUT OF THE BOX

In our times, most people in Western civilization are likely to find it difficult to accept a cyclical view of the universe. This was the dispiriting conclusion of Gertrude Shirk after forty years of promoting this view as research director of the Foundation for the Study of Cycles and editor of its magazine. "A lot of people are very turned off by the concept of rhythmic behavior," she told me. "It's the twentieth-century hubris; we control things."

This form of hubris, which is defined as overweening pride, self-confidence, or arrogance, may have been implanted in the human psyche by the Bible-based religions—Christianity, Judaism, and Islam—that imply a human-centered universe and a mechanistic science that promises to deliver nature into humankind's hand. In both of these traditions, time is viewed as linear, unrepeatable, angled upward in the direction of something called progress or salvation. Matter is measurable and malleable in accordance with determinable causes and effects. There may be cycles, to be sure, but they are cogs in the machine rather than the sources of its power and its determining factors.

Shirk's efforts were not wasted as she seemed to fear. The fact that the basis for man's hubris is gradually being undermined by the very science that helped put it in place can be seen as a cycle in itself. Cycles of doubt, discovery, conviction, and doubt again are clearly observable in the history of science. The current doubt cycle that began with Einstein's challenge to the fervent faith placed in Newtonian physics is still rolling along, and the science of cycles is one of its motivating forces. In fact, the students of cycles might well contend that, in their particular phase of science in general, they have rolled through doubt into discovery and are approaching conviction. Studiers of cycles shake the tower of hubris by claiming that the natural universe operates in a dynamic but rhythmic way; that humans, whose inner rhythms are related to outer rhythms, are an integral part of this natural universe; that humans are, therefore, controlled rather than controlling; that the end of wisdom is to seek a greater understanding of natural forces in order to work with them instead of defying them.

It is clear that getting hooked on cycles can be more than a matter of finding a way of thinking about which stock to buy or what mood you are likely to be in next week. These very practical uses of cycle thinking can be personally rewarding and even socially responsible as in the case of avoiding driving while sleepy. But the philosophical effect of cycle thinking is disruptive of comfortable certitudes and values. Edward S. Dewey said, "If those people who believe in cycle theory are correct, the world operates differently from what most people think. If my father was correct, for instance, every economist, is wrong—and that's just for openers. They are cause and effect people, and he thought that was wrong." Cycle enthusiasts, like basic researchers in other forms of science, tend to describe their change in thinking in terms reminiscent of religious conversion. Typical is Dr. Horovitz's "sense of what *everything* is about" and Roy Tomes's "interrelatedness of all things."

One reason that learning about cycles changes everything is that they are seen to be in everything. Cycles as a science is necessarily interdisciplinary, encompassing not only what are usually thought of as sciences—physics, chemistry, biology, etc.—but also other branches of knowledge such as mathematics, medicine, history, economics, and psychology. This means that the study of cycles is isolated from the ordinary academic channels of thought. Scholars isolated in their own disciplines may never consider cycles a factor to take into account, and neither will practitioners trained by these scholars. Added to hubris, this isolation can account for a general lack of understanding and appreciation for the roles that cycles play in the drama of natural and human life.

Given this background, the welcome that cycle believers extend to fellow apostates is to be expected. The master list of the Foundation for the Study of Cycles' library books runs to thirty-eight pages. Many of the volumes on that list were written by people thinking out of the box about the nature of the universe. In this context, it is fascinating to note that the very first book on the list is *Scientific Heritage of N. Kondratiev* by L. Abalkin. It is a cautionary tale of the very high price original thinkers in an unaccepting society too often pay. Esteemed in cycle circles for identifying a long wave in economic life, still known as the Kondratiev wave, Kondratiev was a loyal communist hoping to renovate the Soviet economy with his idea when he was charged with being a "restorator of capitalism," in 1930 and imprisoned until September 17, 1938, when he was shot by a firing squad. Fortunately, neglect is the only punishment meted out so far to authors of most books dealing with the new frontiers in science. Although cycles are not specifically considered in many of these works, a lot of common ground is discernible in a shared attitude about the need for interdisciplinary approaches and holistic thinking. Because cycles are likely to come into their own as part of a larger movement, it is important to have a look at some of these other thinkers who are considered allies. I make no pretense of doing justice to the brilliant arguments and depth of research in any of the works I cite. My only intent is to show that there is a new wind rising—or a new cycle turning, if you like—in the scientific realm, of which we all should be aware.

Entropy: A New World View by Jeremy Rifkin with Ted Howard

Entropy is a corollary to the second law of thermodynamics. The first law of thermodynamics states that there is a fixed amount of energy which can be transformed from one form to another to accomplish work—as in electricity turned into heat or heat turned into steam; the second law states that, in the transformation process, some energy will be rendered useless for performing future work. Entropy is the measure of this loss of utility. Another way of stating the second law of thermodynamics is to say that everything has a tendency to move from order to disorder, and entropy is the measure of disorder. In this book, the authors make an impassioned case for the proposition that what they call the Entropy Law "remains the only law of science that seems to make common sense out of the world we live in and provides an explanation of how to survive within it."

In their view, the jury is still out on the case for cyclical theory, which they define as a belief that when an expanding universe reaches maximum entropy it will contract itself back to a more ordered state and then re-explode to create another expanding universe and continue the process in endless waves. This, of course, is not necessarily the belief of cycle students, who are more concerned with cycles as a functioning characteristic of the universe as we experience it than an answer to those ultimate questions of its beginning and end. But where the authors of *Entropy* are in agreement with cycle people is evident from the following assertion:

> The old Newtonian view that treats all phenomena as isolated components of matter, or fixed stocks, has given away to the idea that everything is part of a dynamic flow. Classical physics, which recognized only two kinds of classifications, things that exist and things that don't exist, has been challenged and overthrown. Things don't just "exist" as some kind of isolated fixed stock. This static view of the world has been replaced by the view that everything in the world is always in the process of becoming. Even non-living phenomena are continually changing. . . . How different this scientific view is from Newtonian physics with its simple matter in motion, its fixed forces acting against other fixed forces in precise and predictable ways. It's no accident that a science based on manipulating fixed stocks is being replaced by a science based on understanding dynamic flows.

Another point of agreement is that the authors find a form of hubris standing in the way of seeing the truth. In their case, the hubris is pride in technology. Those still imbued with the belief that everything can be reduced to mechanics look to ever-increasing feats of technology to repeal the Law of Entropy—that is, to control the tendency toward the kind of disorder that can be observed, say, in the spread of pollution. What they forget, argue the authors, is the enormous entropy involved in the energy transfer demanded by technology. This is especially true with respect to fossil fuels. In fact, the book illustrates the Law of Entropy in terms of burning a piece of coal. No energy is "lost"; the heat is used for work, and the rest is transformed into sulfur dioxide and other gases. These dissipate in space and add to entropy, or disorder, because the gases cannot be returned to the ordered, usable state of a piece of coal. Thus, the technology in which we take such pride is killing the Earth through entropy at an ever increasing rate. The reverse side of entropy can be seen in living things. Energy, mostly from the Sun, creates order out of disorder in the process of developing plants, animals, and people. Although entropy is created in this process, too, more energy remains in a usable form, and that form is renewable through reproduction. The idea that usable energy is saved as the result of machines doing work that a person can do is totally wrong in this view.

The authors make the case for entropy sounds very much like the case for cycles when they write that "our survival and the survival of all other forms of life now depend on our willingness to make peace with nature and begin to live cooperatively with the rest of our ecosystem. If we do so, and allow the natural recycling process the time it needs to heal the wounds we have inflicted on Earth, then we and all other forms of life can expect a long and healthy sojourn on this planet." It is not a case that is likely to be more popular or more readily accepted than acknowledging uncontrollable rhythms because it demands a rejection of the popular concept of progress as an increase in technical expertise and material wealth.

Global Mind Change by Willis Harman

The relevance of this thought-provoking book to cycle thinking is that it constitutes a strong plea for a more holistic science. The author, whose background includes a professorship in engineering-economic systems at Stanford University, also argues that the mechanistic science of the last several hundred years is no longer acceptable. He, too, sees the attitude that it creates as self-defeating hubris. "Our exuberant Western attitude that all of nature is here to be exploited for our ends may have to be replaced by a far more humble stance if we are to learn from the universe what it would teach us," he writes.

Harman claims that "science has a long history of defending the bulwarks against the persistent reports of phenomena and experiences that 'don't fit it'—such as the spiritual and religious, the exceptionally creative and intuitive, the 'miraculous' in healing and regeneration, the paranormal, seemingly teleologically motivated and instinctual patterns, etc." But now Harman would like to see science "assume the validity of any type of human experience or extraordinary ability which is consistently reported down through the ages, or across cultures, and adapt science in such a way as to accommodate all of these."

One experience that doesn't "fit in," although it was undergone by thousands of people in seminars conducted in both Europe and America, is fire walking, according to Harman. Having internalized the thought that no harm will come to them, participants walk barefoot across coals heated 1,200 to 1,400 degrees Fahrenheit with no pain or harm. "Skeptics have claimed that there is a 'physical' explanation such as low heat conductivity of charcoal, insulating layer of ash, 'leidenfrost effect' of a thin layer of evaporated perspiration," Harman writes. He asserts:

> But whatever the intermediating mechanism, the fact remains when people change the unconscious belief that burning coals will barbecue the feet, they are insulated from harm; change the belief back again and severe third-degree burns can result. The experience is powerful because any doubter can experiment by changing the belief and suffering the painful result. . . . The fundamental fact, powerful and empowering in its implications, is that our experiencing of reality is strongly affected by our internalized beliefs. Our beliefs, in turn, are affected by our experiencing of what we perceive as reality—which most of the time reinforces the beliefs. When it doesn't, we generally feel very uncomfortable—and may be on the way to learning something valuable.

Like cycle students, Harman sees a connectedness in everything in the universe. He calls for "an awareness of the finiteness and multi-interconnectedness of the planetary ecosystem, the inextricable interdependence of all human communities and dependence on the planetary life-support systems." Probably for much the same reason that Edward R. Dewey wanted to see cycles incorporated into scientific study, Harman feels that the mind change to the holistic view he advocates—"the whole is qualitatively different from the sum of its parts"—should take place among scientists.

"We in modern society give tremendous prestige and power to our official, publicly validated knowledge system, named science. It is unique in this position; none of the coexisting knowledge systems—not any system of philosophy or theology, nor philosophy or theology as a whole—is in a comparable position," Harmon writes. "It is impossible to create a well-working society on a knowledge base which is fundamentally inadequate, seriously incomplete, and mistaken in basic assumptions. Yet this is precisely what the modern world has been trying to do."

Harmon's thinking is very much in tune with that of Leslie Botha, one of the most prominent twenty-first century cycle thinkers. Both call for greater harmony with nature and suggest reviving the wisdom to be found in so-called primitive societies. In relation to environmental concerns, Harmon reminds readers that "in some cases (for example, many American Indian tribes) there has always been a clear tradition of caring for the Earth." In her effort to curtail artificial tampering with the natural menstrual cycle, Botha reported on societies in which the cycle was so revered that it made "goddesses" of women.

Harmon and Botha would be in agreement, as well, on the role that patriarchal and industrialized societies have played in creating a dangerous disharmony in relations not only with nature but among human beings. Artificial suppression of the menstrual cycle can be seen as an aspect of male dominance and the man-made time demands of the workplace, according to Botha. Harmon wrote of an "emerging vision" in the global mind that:

emphasizes community in the small view, and global cooperation in the large. Institutions will be more person-centered, and non-discriminatory with regard to sex, race, and culture. One of the most important shaping forces is the rebalancing of masculine and feminine influences. The most powerful of the forces shaping the modern world—reductionist science and manipulative technology, competitive enterprise, the aggressive nation-state—were strongly biased toward masculine and patriarchal perspectives. Implicit in the [global mind] assumptions is an emphasis on wholeness, involving a creative balance between masculine and feminine qualities—between aggressiveness and nurturing, competition and cooperation, rationality and intuition. Riane Eisler, in *The Chalice and the Blade* speaks of the change as being from a "dominator" model of society (which predominated in the West for around 5,000 years) to a "partnership" model.

Chaos: Making a New Science by James Gleick

As with entropy, the science of chaos—if it yet exists—does not endorse cycles specifically. Because, by definition, it is concerned with irregularities that keep cropping up in every system, it would seem to constitute a rejection of the cyclical view. Indeed, there is almost a sneering tone about cycles in this passage from Gleick's book: "Why do investors insist on the existence of cycles in gold and silver prices? Because periodicity is the most complicated orderly behavior they can imagine. When they see a complicated pattern of prices, they look for some periodicity wrapped in a little random noise. And scientific experimenters, in physics or chemistry or biology, are no different."

But believers in chaos and believers in cycles would be on the same side in arguing that the concept of a nature made up of static linear systems has got to go. Gleick quotes atomic scientist Enrico Fermi as saying, "It does not say in the Bible that all laws of nature are expressible linearly!" In addition to subscribing to a conviction that all systems are dynamic, both sets of believers recognize the global nature of systems and the need for an interdisciplinary approach to understand them. As Gleick said of chaos believers, "They feel that they are turning back a trend in science toward reductionism, the analysis of systems in terms of their constituent parts: quarks, chromosomes, or neurons. They believe that they are looking for a whole."

But Gleick's book is probably in the library of the Foundation for the Study of Cycles because Dr. Horovitz saw an affinity between the two approaches to truth that may have escaped others. One definition of cycles is patterns, and, paradoxically, the science of chaos is discerning its own kind of patterns in the universe. As Dr. Horovitz explained to me:

> Fractal relationships from this new science called chaos are related to what we are doing. It's kind of our domain. A fractal is a dimensional relationship. If you take a map of Long Island, for example, and reduce it in size by 1,000 you would still have the same edge to it. It's recurring patterns at dimensional leaps. An electron spinning around the nucleus of an atom is an orbital fractal dimension. The next level up is the Moon spinning around the Earth, the next fractal dimension. The next level up is the planet spinning around the Sun, and then you have the solar system spinning around the center of the galaxy, and then you have all these galaxies spinning around the center of what we believe is a super galaxy. Then we think the super galaxy spins with other galaxies around a hub. Also the science of chaos helps you develop probabilities for things we used to think were random. Science is saying there is less randomness.

The Ages of Gaia by **James Lovelock**

"Because of the tribalism that isolates the denizens of the scientific disciplines, biologists who made models of the competitive growth of the species chose to ignore the physical and chemical environment. Geochemists who made models of the cycles of the elements, geophycists who modeled the climate, chose to ignore the dynamic interaction of the species. As a result, their models, no matter how detailed, are incomplete."

These words of Lovelock, a British generalist in the sciences, should sound familiar. He was obviously a member of the growing group of thinkers in revolt against the parochialism of the sciences as they are still generally taught and practiced. From my reading of him, Lovelock's look at the workings of the universe did not preclude a significant role for cycles. His concern was to get across the concept he called "Gaia"—the Earth and its surrounding atmosphere—is a single living entity. A sense of his vision comes through in the following passage:

> Gaia as the largest manifestation of life differs from other living organisms of Earth in the way that you or I differ from our population of living cells. At some early time in the Earth's history before life existed, the solid Earth, the atmosphere, and oceans were still evolving by the laws of physics and chemistry alone. It was careening downhill, to the lifeless steady state of a planet almost at equilibrium. Briefly, in its headlong flight through the ranges of chemical and physical states, it entered a stage favorable for life. At some special time in that stage, the newly formed living cells grew until their presence so affected Earth's environment as to halt the headlong dive towards equilibrium. At that instant, the living things, the rocks, the air, and the oceans merged to form

the new entity, Gaia. Just as when the sperm merges with the egg, new life was conceived.

This life within Gaia has acted as an automatic regulator—analogous to a household heating system governed by a thermostat—to keep the environment livable by curbing extremes. All forms of life modify the environment. For example, animals change the atmosphere by breathing, taking in oxygen and letting out carbon dioxide, while plants do the reverse. This has counteracted or at least delayed the buildup of entropy which ultimately results in equilibrium, or death. Because the life cycle *is* a cycle and the home heating analogy is often used to describe the function of cycles, the concept of Gaia goes well with that of cycles.

The Body Electric: Electromagnetism and the Foundation of Life by Robert O. Becker, M.D., and Gary Selden

Dr. Becker, a surgeon, started out with a theory that the electrical current in wounds—what he called the "current of injury"—stimulated regeneration and healing. In the process of investigating and testing this theory he crossed the boundary of scientific specialties to develop a much broader view of the function of electricity in animating the universe. Although he did not deal with cycles per se, I do cite some of Dr. Becker's discoveries in support of the theory among some cycle students that electromagnetism might be the crossover force that accounts for such phenomena as identical rhythms in celestial bodies and human activities.

Whether this turns out to be true or not, Dr. Becker's thinking is certainly in accord with that of cycle proponents. Like them, he took the posi-

tion that the dynamic, interrelated systems of the universe can be understood only through a holistic approach. He summoned a potent witness
for his case in the form of Albert Szent-Györgyi, winner of a Nobel Prize
for work in oxidation and vitamin C. Speaking at a meeting of the Buda-
pest Academy of Science in 1941, Szent-Györgyi deplored the mechanistic
approach of biochemistry on the grounds that, when experimenters broke
things down into component parts, life slipped through their fingers and
left them staring at dead matter. "It looks as if some basic fact about life was
still missing, without which any real understanding is impossible," said the
Nobel laureate, according to Dr. Becker. Szent-Györgi thought that the salient fact might be electricity, but his realization that something was missing
in much of scientific thinking also makes his remarks relevant to the claims
of cycle advocates.

It seems impossible to stand on the frontier of science without a vision
beckoning. Dr. Becker's vision incorporates elements of many of the others,
and it has the advantage of being grounded, so to speak, in electricity, a force
that most of us understand from daily experience. Here, in his own words:

> Over and over again biology has found that the whole is more
> than the sum of its parts. We should expect that the same is true
> of bioelectromagnetic fields. All life on Earth can be considered
> a unit, a glaze of sentience spread thinly over the crust. *In toto* its
> field would be a hollow, invisible sphere inscribed with a trac-
> ery of all the thoughts and emotions of all creatures. The Jesuit
> priest and paleontologist-philosopher Pierre Teilhard de Chardin
> postulated the same thing, a noosphere, or ocean of the mind,
> arising from the biosphere like a spume. Given a biological com-
> munications channel that can circle the whole earth in an instant,

possibly based on life's very mode of origin, it would be a wonder if each creature had not retained a link with some such aggregated mind. If so, the perineural DC system [current in the nerves] could lead us to the great reservoir of image and dreams variously called the collective unconscious, intuition, the pool of archetypes, higher intelligences deific or satanic, the Muse herself.

The Lightness of Being: Mass, Ether, and the Unification of Forces by **Frank Wilczek**

I have to confess that the many elaborate equations scattered throughout this book are beyond my comprehension. But they would doubtless be things of beauty for a mathematician, and what the author has learned about the structure of the universe through these equations does relate to cycles thinking. He states flatly that "essentially new forces rule the nuclear world" and concludes:

> Looking down on the valley of everyday reality, we perceive much more than before. Beneath the familiar, sober appearances of enduring matter in empty space, our mind envisions the dance of intricate patterns within a pervasive, ever-present, effervescent medium. We perceive that mass, the very quality that renders matter sluggish and controllable, derives from the energy of quarks and gluons ever moving at the speed of light, compelled to huddle together to shield one another from the buffeting of that medium. Our substance is the hum of a strange music, a mathematical music more precise and complex than a Bach fugue, the Music of the Grid.

As of this writing, this vision of what goes on in atomic nuclei could only be seen in the equations. "The obvious difficulty is simply that it is hard to observe those equations at work, because atomic nuclei are very small," according to Wilczek. "They are roughly a hundred thousand times smaller even than atoms. This takes us a million times beyond nanotechnology. Nuclei are in the domain of micro-nanotechnology. In trying to manipulate nuclei with macroscopic tools—say, to set the scale, an ordinary tweezer—we're worse off than some giant trying to pick up a grain of sand using a pair of Eiffel towers for chopsticks. It's a tough job. To explore the nuclear domain, wholly new experimental techniques had to be invented, and exotic kinds of instruments constructed."

The building of one of these instruments provided *New York Times* essayist Dennis Overbye with a salient point in extolling President Obama's inaugural promise to "restore science to its rightful place." Overbye argued that true democracy and the kind of thinking out of the box required by science go hand in hand, as in this passage:

> Science is not a monument of received Truth but something that people do to look for truth. That endeavor, which has transformed the world in the last few centuries, does indeed teach values. Those values, among others, are honesty, doubt, respect for evidence, openness, accountability and tolerance and indeed hunger for opposing points of view. These are the unabashedly pragmatic working principles that guide the buzzing, testing, poking, probing, argumentative, gossiping, gadgety, joking, dreaming and tendentious cloud of activity—the writer and biologist Lewis Thomas once likened it to an anthill—that is slowly and thoroughly penetrating every nook and cranny of the world.
>
> Nobody appeared in a cloud of smoke and taught scientists these virtues. This behavior simply evolved because it worked.

It requires no metaphysical commitment to God or any conception of human origin or nature to join in this game, just the hypothesis that nature can be interrogated and that nature is the final arbiter. Jews, Catholics, Muslims, atheists, Buddhists and Hindus have all been working side by side building the Large Hadron Collider and its detectors these last few years. And indeed there is no leader, no grand plan, for this hive as much on the Internet and in airport coffee shops as in any one place or time. Or at least it is as utopian as any community largely dependent on government and corporate financing can be. Arguably, science is the most successful human activity of all time.

A Brief History of Time by Stephen W. Hawking

Considered by many to be the greatest theoretical physicist since Einstein, Hawking occupies the same chair as did Isaac Newton as Lucasian Professor of Mathematics at Cambridge University in England—something of an irony in view of the challenge his thinking poses to Newtonian law. Much of Hawking's book, which became an astonishing bestseller, is devoted to showing how inadequate various theories developed throughout history, including some of his own, have proved to be, and still are, in giving a complete picture of the universe. That the study of cycles might eventually provide such a picture was the hope of Edward R. Dewey. Although Hawking's rather healthy skepticism raises doubt as to whether the human mind will ever achieve that goal, there is a strong suggestion that the efforts being made through quantum mechanics and cycle study have much in common.

Discoveries of ever more regularities and laws of nature over the last 300 years of developing civilization led to what Hawking calls "scientific determinism—that there would be a set of laws that would determine the evolution of the universe precisely, given its configuration at one time." But the uncertainty principle of quantum mechanics—"that certain pairs of quantities, such as the position and velocity of a particle, cannot both be predicted with complete accuracy"—has done away with the hope of arriving at such a comfortable understanding. Bearing in mind that waves can be cycles, consider Hawking's description of quantum mechanics's response to the uncertainty principle:

> Quantum mechanics deals with this situation via a class of quantum theories in which particles don't have well-defined positions and velocities but are represented by a wave. These quantum theories are deterministic in the sense that they give laws for the evolution of the wave with time. Thus if one knows the wave at one time, one can calculate it at any other time. The unpredictable, random element comes in only when we try to interpret the wave in terms of the positions and velocities of particles. But maybe that is our mistake; maybe there are no particle positions and velocities, but only waves. It is just that we try to fit the waves to our preconceived ideas of positions and velocities. The resulting mismatch is the cause of the apparent unpredictability. In effect, we have redefined the task of science to be the discovery of laws that will enable us to predict events up to the limits set by the uncertainty principle.

For all practical purposes, the uncertainty principle means that humans will have to live by the probabilities we can determine, and in this a knowledge of cycles can be a helpful guide. But even if the shaking of the scientific foundation under the tower of hubris brings it crashing down, the idea that cycles are in control of human affairs will meet heavy resistance. What about humankind's supposed free will, for instance? Cycle proponents argue that the existence and function of cycles is no greater limit to freedom than is acknowledging the authority of the law of gravity by not jumping from a ten-story window. The use of free will comes into play in making the right choices when confronted with probabilities presented by a knowledge of cycles. John Bagby, for example, was not *forced* by his belief in a rhythmic return of earthquqakes in California to build his house on a rock and undergo the rigors of a long commute instead of easing life by taking the risk of living elsewhere. Not even the wildest enthusiast argues that cycles per se are overwhelming. Although a cycle may be beyond human control, the consequences of its rhythmic recurrence may not be. Fergus Wood could forecast potentially dangerous high tides a century in advance, and no human can change that script. The tide will surely arrive almost to the minute, but the engineering ingenuity of humans is such that shoreline facilities could be built in such a way as to make the tide's arrival of little or no consequence.

In spite of the uncertainty principle, the determinism implicit in cyclical thinking has many ideological and philosophical overtones. Geologist Rhodes Fairbridge thought that a tendency to shy away from determinism goes back in history to a rejection of the concept that everything is determined by God—a concept that understandably lost ground with scholars when the church tried to enforce its views, for example, having the Inquisition sentence Galileo to house arrest for life. "But to substitute nature for God is not a leap that most people with that attitude are prepared to make," Fairbridge said. Except for those few who still cling to a human-centered view of the universe, there would appear to be ample room these days for both God and nature in a universe of cycles. In the interval since scholarship finally broke free of religious control and censorship, most theologians have accepted the continuing discoveries of science as an unfolding of knowledge about how God's creation works. In that sense, cycles would be just another manifestation of the mysterious ways in which God performs wonders.

There is room for doubt and an open mind in cycleland, too. Like all other scientific theories postulated so far, the theory that cycles might be the clue to solving the ultimate mystery of creation is far from proved. The test for the validity of a scientific theory is the ability to make predictions that hold up under experimentation and/or observation. As we have seen, cycle theory does well on this test. But its score is so far from perfect that the users of cycles prefer to speak of advisories and probabilities instead of forecasts and predictions. In this, too, they would appear to be on the cutting edge of science. Talk of calling a whole new science "chaos"—a state of things in which chance is supreme, according to *Webster's*—is enough to indicate how a new humility is gaining ground as unpredictable irregularities surface in supposedly smooth systems when subjected to ever closer scrutiny.

Einstein, also in search of a unified theory, was not fond of the uncertainty principle because it ran counter to his famous statement that "God does not play dice with the universe." On the other hand, the uncertainty principle seen from a theological or philosophical point of view allows God to intervene in the clockwork operation of creation in the form of irregularities. A theorist of chaos, Joseph Ford, responded to Einstein by saying, "God plays dice with the universe, but they're loaded dice. And the main objective of physics now is to find out by what rules were they loaded and how can we use them for our own ends." It sounds a lot like what cycle people are trying to do through their own discipline.

Despite the fact that his theory of relativity changed humanity's relationship to the universe, Einstein could be wrong, and one of his endearing traits was that he was often the first to admit it. Einstein was as humble in person as in mind. I used to see him wandering through the campus of Princeton University, sockless feet in tennis shoes, sweat-shirted, white hair blowing in disarray, licking an ice cream cone and obviously lost in thought. With that vision in mind, it did not surprise me to come upon this prayer-like acknowledgment of awe in contemplation of the universe in Einstein's *The World As I See It*:

> The fairest thing we can experience is the mysterious. It is the fundamental emotion which stands at the cradle of true art and true science. He who knows it not and can no longer wonder, no longer feel amazement, is as good as dead, a snuffed out candle. It was the experience of mystery—even if mixed with fear—that engendered religion. A knowledge of the existence of something we cannot penetrate, of the manifestations of the profoundest reason and the most radiant beauty, which are only accessible to our reason in their most elementary forms—it is this knowledge and this emotion that constitute the truly religious attitude; in this sense and in this alone, I am a deeply religious man. . . . Enough for me the mystery of the eternity of life, and the inkling of the marvelous structure of reality, together with the single-hearted endeavor to comprehend a portion, be it ever so tiny, of the reason that manifests itself in nature.

AFTERWORD

WILL IT ALL END THIS WAY?

Chalk the intriguing figure 12/21/12 on your memory board. Spelled out, it signifies the month—December—the date—twenty-first—and the year—2012 when history as we know it on Earth will come to an end in the belief of thousands of people the world around. No book on cycles written in 2009 should overlook this belief, because it is based on cycles with a 5,125-year cycle at its core. Alerting their fellow human beings to an event of such magnitude has grown over the last twenty years into a New Age enterprise involving numerous articles, books, films; radio, TV, Internet appearances; and sales of caps, buttons, and T-shirts. Perhaps because its advocates and adherents are for the most part out of the box thinkers, there has been little attention paid to their warning in the mainstream media.

The first alarm, if that is the proper term, was sounded in 1987 by José Argüelles, Ph.D., in a book called *The Mayan Factor: Path Beyond Technology*. Author of four other books, Argüelles earned his doctorate in art history and aesthetics at the University of Chicago and taught at Princeton University and the San Francisco Art Institute, among others. He founded Planet Art Network and the Foundation for the Law of Time. Before encountering the ancient Mayan civilization and its end-time prediction, Argüelles was involved in the study and practice of Eastern religions, as he writes:

> I found in the Tibetan Buddhist teachings a major grounding for my mind. Throwing myself intensely into the meditation practices made available to me through my teacher, Chogyam Trungpa Rinpoche, I found in the Vajrayana teachings a context for my continuing investigations of things Mayan. In particular, the teachings of mind-only seemed most useful for further considerations of the Mayan calendar, its origins and especially its philosophical or scientific basis. Like the Buddhist (and Hindu) cosmologies, the Mayan describes a universe of infinite cycles of time and being. If anything, the Mayan is even more precise in its computations of these cycles. In any case, the contemplation of the far-ranging and all-encompasing cycles inevitably led to a consideration of the fact that we are not alone, that infinite other world systems exist more evolved than that of our own system.

Although the word *Maya* now denotes indigenous inhabitants of Central America, Argüelles found it resounds through many lands and all history. Buddha's mother was named Maya, as was one of the famous Hindu astrologers. In Hindu philosophy, *Maya* is a term for "origin of the world." In Egypt, king Tutankhamen's treasurer was known as Maya. There was a girl called Maia among the daughters of Atlas in Greek mythology, and the month of May comes from the Roman goddess of spring, Maia. The Yucatan Peninsula, where a group of wanderers settled after crossing the Bering Strait from Asia in an ice age some 12,000 years ago was once known as Mayab. It was a long time in coming, but the Maya created an impressive civilization that lasted for 500 years before their cities were mysteriously abandoned by A.D. 830 and left to crumble in the jungle.

During a decade or more of wide reading, Argüelles found himself fascinated with the hieroglyphs the Mayans left behind on the ruins. They revealed amazing scientific achievements without aid of instruments other than the human eye and mind:

> The Maya computed the length of the Earth's revolution around the Sun to within a thousandth of a decimal point of the calculations of modern science. . . . Not only that, but they kept calendars of the lunation and eclipse cycles; and even more, they maintained calendars recording synodical revolutions and synchronizations of the cycle of Mercury, Venus, Mars, Jupiter, and Saturn. And, on certain monuments, we find the recording of dates and/or events occurring as much as 400,000,000 years in the past. All of this they did with a unique and incredibly simple yet flexible numerical system that counted by twenties (instead of tens) and used only three notational symbols.

In this light, Argüelles did not find it difficult to take seriously the so-called Great Cycle of the Mayans, beginning at 3113 B.C. and ending on that intriguing date in 2012.

In his book, Argüelles goes much deeper into Mayan cosmology and the cyclical nature of the universe it depicts. He finds a harmonic resonance at work in these cycles:

If this world view sounds Pythagorean—music of the spheres—it is! Yet the difference between the Pythagoreans and the Maya is this: the Maya demonstrated to no uncertain degree that this is not merely a philosophy but the basis of an entire civilization. Such a civilization based on the principle of harmonic resonance is obviously different in nature and purpose than a civilization such as ours, which is based on the acquisition of material goods and defense of territory.

When Argüelles's book appeared, 12/21/12 seemed comfortably far away. But that last figure took on something of an urgency with the turn to a new millennium, and a number of self-appointed Mayan scholars made it their business to look into the mysterious matters raised by the "Mayan factor." One of them, Lawrence E. Joseph, author of *Apocalypse 2012: A Scientific Investigation into Civilization's End* was refreshingly honest about his approach to the task. "I am not New Agey," he writes. "I am your basic Brooklyn wiseguy Beeming around Beverly Hills. Not that all that ancient oojie-boojie is necessarily invalid, just that most of it is lost on me. . . . I represent no religious or political ideology nor have I, to the very best of my knowledge fallen under the influence of any individual or group with views relating to 2012."

In keeping with these acknowledgments is what Joseph calls "the thesis" of his book:

> 1. Ancient Mayan prophesies based on two millennia of meticulous astronomical observations indicate that 12/21/12 will mark the birth of a new age, accompanied as all births are, by blood and agony as well as hope and promise.

2. Since the 1940s and particularly since 2003, the Sun has behaved more tumultuously than any time since the rapid global warming that accompanied the melting of the last Ice Age 11,000 years ago. Solar physicists concur that solar activity will next peak, at record-setting levels, in 2012.

3. Storms on the Sun are related to storms on Earth. The great wave of 2005 hurricanes Katrina, Rita, and Wilma coincided with one of the stormiest weeks in the recorded history of the Sun.

4. The Earth's magnetic field, our primary defense against harmful solar radiation, has begun to dwindle, with California-sized cracks opening randomly. A pole shift, in which such protection falls nearly to zero as the North and South magnetic poles reverse position, may well be under way.

5. Russian geophysicists believe that the solar system has entered an interstellar energy cloud. This cloud is energizing and destabilizing the Sun and all the planets' atmospheres. Their predictions for catastrophe resulting from Earth's encounter with this energy cloud range from 2010 to 2020.

6. Physicists at UC–Berkeley, who discovered that the dinosaurs and 70 percent of all other species on Earth were extinguished by the impact of a comet or asteroid 65 million years ago, maintain with 99 percent certainty, that we are now overdue for another such megacastastrophe.

7. The Yellowstone supervolcano, which erupts catastrophically every 600,000 to 700,000 years, is preparing to blow. The most recent eruption of comparable magnitude, at Lake Toba, Indonesia, 74,000 years ago led to the death of more than 90 percent of the world's population at that time.

8. Eastern philosophies, such as the I Ching, the Chinese Book of Changes, and Hindu theology, have been plausibly interpreted as supporting the 2012 end date, as have a range of indigenous belief systems.

9. At least one scholarly interpretation of the Bible predicts that the Earth will be annihilated in 2012. The burgeoning Armageddonist movement of Muslims, Christians, and Jews actively seeks to precipitate the final-end-times battle.

10. Have a nice day.

Joseph supports the points he makes in his thesis with abundant and distressing facts and figures. About the Yellowstone supervolcano, for instance, he reports that in its last known eruption 640,000 years ago, it spewed enough ash into the atmosphere to spread a blanket of soot and cinders one meter deep across the entire United States and block out sunlight for nearly a decade. With the cycle due to return, it was not good news when NASA investigators found a huge caldera in 1993. An underground depression filled with magma, a noxious mixture of solid and liquid rock and volcanic gases, this caldera is, according to Joseph, "the molten, beating heart of Yellowstone Park" that has risen nearly a meter since 1922 and is about to explode. As a sign of this possibility, he cites a report by Robert B. Smith, a geophysicist from the University of Utah, that the bulging caldera has tilted the Yellowstone Lake causing it to drain from its south end.

Although he predicts bloody catastrophe, Joseph is willing to accept the possibility that it could give birth to a new and better existence for those who survive.

Daniel Pinchbeck, author of *2012: The Return of Quetzacoatl*, also accepts this possibility. But his approach to the subject is very different, as stated in his introduction:

This book advances a radical theory: that human consciousness is rapidly transitioning to a new state, a new intensity of awareness that will manifest as a different understanding, a transformed realization of time and space and self. By this thesis, the transition is already under way—though largely subliminally—and will become increasingly evident as we approach the year 2012. According to the sacred calendar of the Mayan and Toltec civilizations of Mesoamerica, this date signifies the end of a "Great Cycle" of more than five thousand years, the conclusion of one world age and the beginning of the next.

Traditionally, the completion of the Great Cycle was associated with the return of the Mesoamerican deity Quetzalcoatl, "Sovereign Plumed Serpent," depicted in sculptures and temple friezes as a fusion of bird and snake, representing the union of spirit and matter. Mexican archaeologist Enrique Florescano writes: "Quetzalcoatl is the god who hands down civilization, reveals time, and discerns the movement of the stars and human destiny." The hypothesis I propose is that the completion of the Great Cycle and the return of Quetzalcoatl are archetypes, and their underlying meaning points toward a shift in the nature of the psyche. If this theory is correct, the transformation of our consciousness will lead to the rapid creation, development, and dissemination of new institutions and social structures, corresponding to our new level of mind. From the limits of our current chaotic and uneasy circumstances, this process may well resemble an advance toward a harmonic, perhaps even utopian, situation on Earth.

It would be a grave sin of oversimplification to try to summarize Pinchbeck's argument for the role of the mind, of the collective consciousness, in the drama of 2012. He calls it "an extravagant thought experiment—a kind of 'no holds barred' poker wager or roulette gamble played in the realm of ideas." But it is a fascinating experiment that leads to an assumption that the Great Cycle might circle back to the creation of civilizations that, in his words:

> lived to a model of time that differs from our contemporary aware-ness of it as a one-way linear extension. They believed that events and epochs inevitably followed a cyclical or spiral pattern, and the development of human societies and human thought was integrat-ed, synchronized, with the immense gyrations of planets, stars, and constellations. For the Mayans and Egyptians and the architects of Stonehenge and Chaco Canyon, astronomy was a sacred science. They built their pyramids and monuments as calendars and obser-vatories, anchoring themselves in relation to the observable cosmos.

Among the signs Pinchbeck investigated of an approaching mind-changing event the most unusual was crop circles—intelligible designs in vegetation that have appeared mysteriously on the continent and in Great Britain. He recounts the tale of a woman named Nancy Talbot who was visiting a Dutch farmhouse while researching the phenomenon. While she was getting ready to go to bed, she was aware of an eerie silence—no sound from the usually noisy dogs and cows and other animals. Looking out the window, she saw a beam of glowing energy hit the ground and fade out. In the morning, she found a circle with a crossed *T* in the middle imprinted in the vegetation as if she had been sent a personal message from on high. In England, a hardheaded architect and industrial designer named Michael Glickman was so intrigued by what he saw in crop circles that he retired to devote his time to studying them. He was convinced after a decade of study that they were messages from a "prodigious intelligence" monitoring the evolution of consciousness on Earth. In 1997 he read the intent of a large grid square within a circle—twenty six rows of thirty squares—as a "map of time." The total of squares equaled the number of weeks remaining from its date of appearance until the last week of 2012.

Pinchbeck quotes another self-appointed Mayan scholar named John Major Jenkins as saying that "around the year 2012, a large chapter in human history will be coming to an end. All the values and assumptions of the previous World Age will expire, and a new phase of human growth will commence. The Maya understood this to be a natural process, in which new life follows death." Jenkins, author of more than half a dozen books and many more articles on Mayan history and culture, became a kind of ring master of all the 2012 apostles, appearing with them on radio, in films, and on stage. He may have been a crowd-pleaser because his message is more positive than most. As he told Benjamin Anastas for an article in the *New York Times Magazine*, "A lot of people are talking about apocalypse right now, but there's a deeper meditation that can and should happen around the end date. At any end-beginning nexus—at the dawn of a new religion or a spiritual tradition—you have this amazing opening. There's a fresh awareness of what it means to be alive in the full light of history."

Jenkins's belief that *something* will happen on or in the neighborhood of 12/21/12 is fittingly based on a reading of the skies. The event will be brought about by the Galactic Alignment—an alignment of the December solstice Sun with the galactic equator which occurs only once every 26,000 years, according to Jenkins's Web site.

"This was what the ancient Maya were pointing to with the 2012 end-date of their Long Count calendar," he writes. Jenkins inspires more credence than some other 2012 prophets because doing the math makes him hedge his own bets by admitting that the Galactic Alignment is only a guarantee of something he calls "era-2012."

All the talk of 2012 has naturally excited the thousands upon thousands of people who believe in an unspecified end-time for religious reasons or because of a pessimistic view of the current state of earthly affairs. In both Christian and Muslim theology there is justification for the religious anticipation of what is known as the rapture—an event associated with the second coming of Christ for Christians and of the Mahdi, the Shiite version of the Messiah. In and around this event to which the faithful look forward with joy in promised salvation, will be some form of prophesied catastrophe such as the battle of Armageddon to rid the world of sin and sinners. Consider the scene in Revelation 16:12-21:

> The sixth angel poured his bowl on the great river Euphrates, and its water dried up, to prepare the way for the kings from the east. And I saw, issuing from the mouth of the beast and from the mouth of the false prophet, three foul spirits like frogs; for they were demonic spirits, performing signs, who go abroad to the kings of the whole world, to assemble them for battle on the great day of God the Almighty. ("Lo, I am coming like a thief! Blessed is he who is awake, keeping his garments that he may not

go naked and be seen exposed!") And they assembled them at the place, which is called in Hebrew Armageddon.

The seventh angel poured his bowl in the air; and a great voice came out of the temple, from the throne saying, "It is done!" And there were flashes of lightning, loud noises, peals of thunder, and a great earthquake such as had never been since men were on earth, so great was that earthquake. The great city was split into three parts, and the cities of the nations fell, and God remembered great Babylon to make her drain the cup of fury of his wrath. And every island fled away, and no mountains were to be found; and great hailstones, heavy as a hundred-weight, dropped on men from heaven, till men cursed God for the plague of the hail, so fearful was that plague.

After many more accounts of destruction to do away with all evil, we come to Revelation 21:1-5:

Then I saw a new heaven and a new earth; for the first heaven and the first earth had passed away, and the sea was no more. And I saw the holy city, new Jerusalem; coming down out of heaven from God, prepared as a bride adorned for her husband; and I heard a great voice from the throne saying, "Behold, the dwelling of God is with men. He will dwell with them, and they shall be his people, and God himself shall be with them; he will wipe away every tear from their eyes, and death shall be no more, neither shall there be mourning nor crying nor pain any more, for the former things have passed away." And he who sat on the throne said, "Behold, I make all things new."

It would not be hard for Biblical believers to hear an echo of that scripture in Jenkins's talk of "a new phase of human growth," or see a reprise in Pinchbeck's "harmonic, perhaps even utopian, situation on Earth." But the scripture for nonbelievers would more likely be found in the Bulletin of the Atomic Scientists' Doomsday Clock Overview on the Internet, and it would be cold comfort. The minute hand of the clock was set at seven minutes to midnight—an end-time of catastrophic destruction—in 1947 because of the existence and spread of atomic weapons, but it was advanced to five minutes left to go in 2007 because of global warming and the development of biological weapons. Because neither atomic nor rocket scientists can predict a definite date, the arguments on behalf of a world changing event on 12/21/12 could be quite appealing to the minds of people who, like Joseph, the "Brooklyn wiseguy," are not into "ancient oojie-boojie" or the New Age. Indeed, the very sober cycles scientist Theodor Landscheidt predicted a period of instability from 2002 to 2011 that "will prove to be another turning point, a period of . . . upheaval, agitation, and revolution that ruins traditional structures, but favors the emergence of new patterns in society, economy, art, and science." Based on his forecast of a transition to a cold period beginning in 2000, historian Wheeler thought that there would be a new renaissance and a "finer and greater democracy than the world has ever known."

In view of the many predictions of dire events on definite days throughout history that didn't come true—Y2K, for instance—there is just cause for skepticism about 12/21/12. Professor Anthony Aveni, increased this skepticism by telling *New York Times* writer Anastas, "I defy anyone to look up into the sky and see the galactic equator. You need a radio telescope for that, and they were not known anywhere in the world that I've heard of until the 1930s." Indeed, there is some question as to what the Mayan savants and their modern disciples see and with what. Both are known to believe in using hallucinogenic drugs to expand the range of vision and consciousness. But, as of this writing, there is no way to know for sure what will happen on 12/21/12. We'll just have to wait and see.

BIBLIOGRAPHY

BOOKS

Abalkin, L. *Scintific Heritage of N. Kondratieve and Contemporaneity.* Moscow: Institute of Economics, Russian Academy of Scientists, 1992.

Arguelles, Jose. *The Mayan Factor: Path Beyond Technology.* Vermont: Bear & Company, 1987.

Ayensu, Edward S., and Dr. Philip Whitfield, eds. *The Rhythms of Life.* New York: Crown Publishers, Inc., 1981.

Becker, Robert O., M.D., and Gary Selden, *The Body Electric.* New York: William Morrow & Co., Inc., 1987.

Boslough, John. *Stephen Hawking's Universe.* New York: William Morrow & Co., Inc., 1985.

Carter, Elizabeth A., and Monica McGoldrick, eds. *The Family Life Cycle.* New York: Gardner Press, Inc., 1980.

Collingwood, R. G. *Essays in the Philosophy of History.* Austin: University of Texas Press, 1965.

Cooley, Donald G. *Predict Your Own Future*. New York: Wilfred Funk, Inc., 1950.

Dewey, Edward R., with Og Mandino. *Cycles*. Portland: Hawthorn Books, 1971.

Dewey, Edward R., and Edwin F. Dakin. *Cycles: The Science of Prediction*, New York: H. Holt and Company, 1947.

Einstein, Albert. *The World As I See It*. New York: Philosophical Library, 1949.

Fairbridge, Rhodes. *Planetary Periodicities and Terrestrial Climate Stress*. Dordrecht: D. Reidel Publishing Company, 1984.

Gleick, James. *Chaos*. New York: Viking, 1987.

Harman, Willis. *Global Mind Change*. Houston: Knowledge Systems, Inc., 1988.

Hawking, Stephen W. *A Brief History of Time*. New York: Bantam Books, 1988.

Horovitz, Jeffrey H., M.D. *The Miracle of Cycles*. Cycles Research Institute, Inc., 2007.

Huntington, Ellsworth. *Mainsprings of Civilization*. New York: John Wiley and Sons, Inc., 1945.

—. *Season of Birth*. New York: John Wiley and Sons, Inc., 1938.

Iacocca, Lee. *Talking Straight*. New York: Bantam Books, 1988.

Joseph, Lawrence E. *Apocalypse 2012*. New York: Random House, 2008.

Jung, C. W. "The Stages of Life" in *The Portable Jung*. New York: Viking, 1971.

Landscheidt, Theodor. *Sun-Earth-Man*. United Kingdom: Urania Trust, 1989.

Levinson, Daniel J., et al. *The Seasons of a Man's Life*. New York: Alfred A. Knopf, 1978.

Lovelock, James. *The Ages of Gaia*. New York: W. W. Norton & Co., 1988.

Luce, Gay Gaer. *Biological Rhythms in Psychiatry and Medicine.* Washington, DC: U.S. Department of Health, Education and Welfare, National Institute of Mental Health, 1970.

Martin, Geoffrey J. *Ellsworth Hungtington.* North Haven: Archon Books, 1973.

Miller, James Grier. *Living Systems.* New York: McGraw-Hill Book Company, 1978.

Moore-Ede, Martin C., Frank M. Sulzman, and Charles A. Fuller. *The Clocks That Time Us.* Cambridge: Harvard University Press, 1982.

Needham, Joseph. *Time and Eastern Man.* London: Royal Anthropological Institute of Great Britain & Ireland, 1964.

Perry, Susan and Jim Dawson. *Secrets Our Body Clocks Reveal.* New York: Rawson Associates, 1988.

Pinchbeck, Daniel. *2012: The Return of Quetzalcoatl.* New York: Tarcher/Penguin, 2006.

Rampino, Michael R., John E. Sanders, Walter S. Newman, and L.K. Konigsson, eds. *Climate History, Periodicity, and Predictability.* New York: Van Nostrand Reinhold Company, 1987.

Rifkin, Jeremy and Ted Howard. *Entropy: A New World View.* New York: Viking Press, 1986.

Ruperti, Alexander. *Cycles of Becoming.* California: CRCS Publications, 1978.

Schlesinger, Arthur M. *Paths to the Present.* New York: Macmillan Co., 1949.

Schlesinger, Arthur M., Jr. *The Cycles of American History.* Boston: Houghton Mifflin Company, 1986.

Schumpeter, Joseph A. *Business Cycles.* New York: McGraw-Hill Book Company, Inc., 1939.

Sheehy, Gail. *Passages.* New York: E. P. Dutton & Co., 1974.

Smith, Edgar Lawrence. *Tides in the Affairs of Men.* New York: Macmillan Co., 1939.

Spiller, Robert E. *The Cycle of American Literature.* New York: Macmillan Co., 1965.

Sze, William C., ed. *Human Life Cycle.* Lanham, MD: Jason Aronson, Inc., 1975.

Thorneycroft, Dr. Terry. *Seasonal Patterns in Business and Everyday Life.* Surrey, UK: Gower, 1987.

Toffler, Alvin. *The Third Wave.* New York: William Morrow & Company, Inc., 1980.

Toynbee, Arnold J. *A Study of History.* England: Oxford University Press, 1947.

Volcker, Paul A. *Rediscovery of the Business Cycle.* New York: Macmillan Publishing Co., 1978.

Wasserman, Harvey. *America Born and Reborn.* New York: Macmillan Publishing Co., 1983.

Wilczek, Frank W. *The Lightness of Being.* New York: Basic Books, 2008.

Williams, William Appleman. *The Contours of American History.* Chicago: Quadrangle Books, 1966.

Wood, Fergus J. *Tidal Dynamics.* New York: Kluwer Academic Publishers, 1986.

Young, A. B. *Recurring Cycles of Fashion.* New York: Harper and Brothers, 1937.

Zahorchak, Michael, ed. *Climate: The Key to Understanding Business Cycles: With a forecast of trends into the 21st century (the Raymond H. Wheeler Papers).* Tide Press, 1983.

PERIODICALS

Abrams, Isabel S. "Beyond Night and Day." *Space World,* December 1986.

"Abstracts." *Chronobiologia,* Organ of the International Society of Chronobiology, XIX International Conference, April/June 1989.

Allan, David G. "On a Sheet of Ice and Under Sail." *New York Times*, February 13, 2009.

Allen, Warren Dwight. "Music History in Five Five-Hundred-Year Cycles." *Journal of Human Ecology* I, no. 13, 1951.

Alpert, Mark. "The Cosmic Apocalypse." *Princeton Alumni Weekly*, February 11, 2009.

Anastas, Benjamin. "The Final Days." *New York Times Magazine*, July 1, 2007.

Ascani, Dan. "Commodities in the Perspective of the Elliott and the Kondratieff Waves." *Cycles*, March/April 1989.

"As the Classic Business Cycle Changes Its Course." *Business Week*, April 4, 1988.

Barron, James. "The 300th Birthday of the Man Who Organized All of Nature." *New York Times*, May 23, 2007.

Bennett, Kelly R. "Seven-Year Spirals." *Cycles*, March 1988.

"Biological Rhythm and Cosmose: The One Commands, the Other Obeys." From *Journal de Geneve*, *Cycles*, May 1970.

Boughton, Cleta Olmstead. "Seasonal Architecture." *Journal of Human Ecology* II, no. 1, 1953.

—. "Seasonal Painting." *Journal of Human Ecology* I, no. 22, 1953.

Brinker, Nancy B. "A 7-Day Cycle in Human Moods." *Cycles*, April 1973.

Brooks, John. "Something Out There." *New Yorker*, February 3, 1962.

Browner, Malcolm W. "Just a Matter of Time." *New York Times Magazine*, September 27, 1987.

Currie, Robert Guinn and Rhodes W. Fairbridge. "Periodic 18.6-Year and Cyclic 11-Year Induced Drought and Flood in Northeastern China and Some Global Implications." *Quaternary Science Review*, 1985.

Dewey, E. R. "Director's Letter." *Cycles*, August 1960.

Eckholm, Erik. "Exploring the Forces of Sleep." *New York Times Magazine*, April 17, 1988.

Epperson, Diane. "Wheeler's 'Big Book'." *Cycles*, January/February 1989.

Fairbridge, Rhodes W. "Prediction of Long-Term Geologic and Climatic Changes that Might Affect the Isolation of Radioactive Waste." *Underground Disposal of Radioactive Wastes* II.

Fairbridge, Rhodes W. and James H. Shirley. "Prolonged Minima and the 179-Year Cycle of the Solar Inertial Motion." *Solar Physics*, 1987.

Hagopian, Ralph V. "Motivations for the Study of Cycles." *Cycles*, August 1967.

Harty, Martha. "A New Approach to Fighting Cancer: Chronochemotherapy." *Cycles*, June 1982.

"Have Services Taken the Sting Out of the Business Cycle?" *Business Week*, April 4, 1988.

Herbst, Anthony F. and Craig W. Slinkman. "Political-Economic Cycles in the U.S. Stock Market." *Financial Analysts Journal*, March/April 1984.

Hersey, Rexford B. "Emotional Cycles in Man." Foundation for the Study of Cycles Reprint from *Journal of Mental Science*, January 1931.

—. "Some Neglected Aspects of Accident Prevention." *Cycles*, January 1952.

Horovitz, Jeffrey H., M.D. "Measuring Your Personal Emotional Cycles." *Cycles*, December 1986.

Huyghe, Patrick. "Science of Cycles." *Science Digest*, August 1983.

"An Inca Stonehenge?" *Cycles*, September 1966.

"Is the World Economy Riding a Long Wave to Prosperity?" *Business Week*, May 5, 1986.

"It's Part of the Legacy of Being Human, Q. & A. with Dr. Henry Schneiderman." *New York Times*, May 7, 1989.

Joquell II, Arthus Louis. "Cycles in Religion." *Cycles*, August 1959.

—. "The Cycle of the World's Great Religions." *Cycles*, April 1959.

Juenemann, Freric B. "The Fifth Force." *Research & Development*, April 1989.

Kane, Michael. "Barron's On Line." April 16, 2008.

Kaulins, Andis. "Cycles in the Birth of Eminent Humans." *Cycles* 30, no. 1 (1979).

Landscheidt, Theodor. "The Creative Function of Cycles." *Cycles*, May/June 1989.

Lee, Dr. Samuel. "Coffee Break." *Tea & Coffee Trade Journal*, September 1982.

"A Light in Time." *Psychology Today*, January 1987.

Lipkin, Richard. "Cycles: Beating to the Same Pulse?" *Insight Magazine*, March 14, 1988.

"The Magnetic Attraction of Periodicities." *Science News*, March 29, 1986.

Marting, Gary. "Political Cycles." *Cycles* 35, 1959.

Matso, Mandy. "Asleep At The Wheel." *Reader's Digest*, April 2002.

"Menstrual Brain Changes Seen." *BBC News*, October 2005.

Merritt, J. I. "Inside the Greenhouse." *Princeton Alumni Weekly*, April 19, 1982.

Mogey, Richard. "The Cycle Outlook for Real Estate." *Cycles*, May/June 1989.

Murphy, Wendy. "Tune To Your Body Clocks." *McCall's*, July 1988.

Nadis, Steve. "Mathematics of Sleep." *Technology Review*, February/March 1987.

Nardone, Diane C. "Is the Movie Industry Contracyclical?" *Cycles*, April 1982.

"New Research on Light Could Be Boon to Sleep." *New York Times*, June 16, 1989.

"The 9-Year Cycle in Social Disease." *Cycles*, July 1958.

O'Malley, Ruth Lynne. "Cycle Semantics." *Executive Report*.

Overbye, Dennis. "Elevating Science, Elevating Democracy." *New York Times*, January 27, 2009.

—. "In Expanding Universe, Stunted Growth." *New York Times*, December 17, 2008.

—. "They Tried to Outsmart Wall Street." *New York Times*, March 10, 2009.

Rampino, Michael R. "Worlds In Collusion." *Cycles*, January/February 1988.

Reid, Tony. "There's a 54-Year Cycle to Rates." *Toronto Sun*, September 4, 1983.

"Researchers Will Use Lasers to Study Earth's Water Cycle." *Earth Science*, Fall 1987.

Reuters. "Signs in Ash of Tsunamis that Struck Centuries Ago." *New York Times*, October 30, 2008.

Roan, Shari. "Defying Gravity." *The Orange County Register*, April 6, 1986.

Roth, Mark. "Foundation Explores Mysterious Rhythms." *Pittsburg Post-Gazette*, July 18, 1983.

"The Seasonal Cycle in Quaker Speaking." *Cycles*, November 1959.

Shirk, Gertrude. "Cycles in Stock Prices—The 40.68-Month Cycle." *Cycles*, March 1987.

—. "Dialogue With a New Member." *Cycles*, November 1966.

—. "What Is It All About?" *Cycles*, March 1962.

Shirley, James H. "When the Sun Goes Backward: Solar Motion, Volcanic Activity and Climate 1990-2000." *Cycles*, March/April 1989.

Siffre, Michel. "The Time of Our Lives." *Unesco Courier*, January 1952.

"Sleeping to the Beat of the Body's Rhythms." *U.S. News and World Report*, June 15, 1987.

"The Solar Inconstant." *Scientific American*, September 1988.

Spitzer, Neil. "Cycles." *The Atlantic*, February 1988.

Stegner, Wallace. "Hydrological Cycles." *Wilderness*, Fall 1987.

Stevens, Sandy. "Hems and Haws." *Cycles*, March 1967.

Stich Kokus, Martin. "Earthquakes, Earth Expansion, and Tidal Cycles." *Cycles*, November 1987.

Stone, W. Clement. "Get On Your Success Cycle." *Success: The Magazine for Achievers*, July 1983.

Styron, William. "Why Primo Levi Need Not Have Died." *New York Times*, December 19, 1988.

Swiss, Dorothy. "A Bundle of Worms." *Cycles*, May/June 1976.

"300,000-year Record of World Temperature." *Cycles*, January 1952.

Vaux, James E. "Cycles in Book Publication." *Cycles*, April 1971.

—. "Possible Cycles in Temperature at Charleston, S.C." *Cycles* XXVI, no. 5.

Wheeler, Raymond Holder. "The Effect of Climate on Human Behavior in History." *Transactions Kansas Academy of Science* 46, 1943.

"Why Does It Rain on January 23?" *Cycles*, August 1960.

Will, George F. "Some Will Take Grim Delight in the New Recession." *International Herald Tribune*, March 1989.

Williams, George E. "The Solar Cycle in Precambrian Time." *Scientific American*, August 1966.

"Writings of Raymond H. Wheeler, Parts 1-10." *Foundation for the Study of Cycles, Inc.*, 1978.

ONLINE RESOURCES

Botha, Leslie. "Happy Hormones Honey—the Greatest Story Never Told." (January 31, 2009). http://holyhormones.com.

"Doomsday Clock Overview."
http://www.thebulletin.org/contents/doomsday-clock/overeview.

Foundation for the Study of Cycles, Inc. http://cycles.cc

Jenkins, John Major. "Alignment 2012." http://alignment2012.cum/about-jmj.html.

"Nobel Peace Prize." (December 6, 2007).
http://research.noaa.edu/news/2007/ipcccontributors.htmc.

"Plate Tectonics." *Wikipedia.* (March 6, 2009).
http://en.wikipedia.org/wiki/plate_tectonics.

"Ray Tomes' Cycles in the Universe." http://ray.tomes.biz.

"Tectonic Plates." (March 6, 2009). http://morlandschool.co.uk/earth/tectonc.htm.